GW00862946

THE DHAMMAKAYA

T. MAGNESS

CONTENTS

SPLIT-SELVES & FRACTURED KARMA

(by Prof. Winston L. King) . . . . I - XIII

THE DHAMMAKAYA 1

IN REPLY TO LETTERS RECEIVED 26

THE GOOD SEED 55

INTRODUCTION

SPLIT—SELVES & FRACTURED KARMA

by

Prof. Winston L. King

Grinnell College, Iowa

SPLIT SELVES AND FRACTURED KARMA

by Prof. Winston L. King

About two years ago quite unexpectedly, I received in the mail one day from Mr. T. Magness of Bangkok—a person totally unknown to me, even though I had spent a full 5 days in Bangkok in 1958—two paper-covered volumes entitled *Samma Ditthi* (Right Understanding) and *Samma Samadhi* (Right Concentration). Immediately, I began to read one of them, being intrigued to find a Theravada Buddhist quoting from Alfred North Whitehead, but then they got somehow displaced from my mainstream of reading. And thus it was not till this past winter that I actually got around to reading them straight through. And not till I was well through my 2nd volume, the *Samma Ditthi*, did I realize that I was encountering something brand new, at least to me, in Theravada Buddhism.

When I discovered this I wrote to Mr. Magness, who promptly and generously gave answers to my questions about this doctrine of split-personality or psychic-offshoots and their relation to the Buddhist doctrines of karma and rebirth. From his books and letters I will attempt to present something of this doctrine.

But first it will be best briefly to present an outline of the basic Buddhist doctrine of selfhood as a background before dealing with the psychic-offshoot doctrine.

I. The Traditional Buddhist Theory of Selfhood

According to this doctrine each of us sentient individuals is one life-moment of an endless chain of life-moments of individualized existence, which has been projecting itself anew, moment by moment, life by life, and age after age, in many forms from some primordial but unspecificable beginning about which Buddhism refuses to speculate. This chain-of-being will continue to project itself forward into an indefinite future eternity, propelled by the blind will-to-be (or *tanha*, the thirst for existence), unless it achieves an absolute detachment from all desire-to-be in some new form, and thus gains Nirvana.

I

This process may be viewed from two somewhat different perspectives. We may take it in *cross - section*, i.e. by an analysis of an existent sentient being at any one moment of its existence. In this perspective Buddhism holds that there is no integral self to be found in the final analysis of self, though of course there *is* an empirically perceptible being - of - sorts. This conviction it states in its doctrine of *anatta*—non-self, no-self,or no-soul. What appears to be a personal individual, says Buddhism, is actually a composite bundle of five loosely related factors, one of *tangible form* (including *physical* form) and four others comprising the feeling, volitional, and consciousness components These have no true center, be it repeated; the so - called persons which we conceive our selves to be, are of *dependent origination*, i.e. formed by the momentary association of our component factors which *together* make up a kind of "person" of illusory substantiality. But this person is never a true unity and comes completely unglued or unwound at physical death. It is more like a stream, to use another favorite Buddhist analogy, which is contained within the rough limits of its banks, i.e. individualized form; but it is really a fluxing, momentarily changing current of mental - physical events, rather than a substance; an "amorphous plurality," to use Mr. Magness' excellent phrase. It is only an impersonal blind will - to - be that thrusts forward from moment to moment and life to life, taking unto itself ever different sets of five-fold factors to form a new pseudo - being at each rebirth.

There is also another way of portraying this essential unreality of the so - called individual being. And this is the doctrine of the "four heaps" or streams of personality. This differs from the above view of the individual as a five - fold bundle of constituent factors, only in emphasis and context, by describing individuality in its formative process. Each heap or stream is one of four *successive* and *causally related* stages of development, but each state, heap, or stream is itself five - fold. And secondarily, in some sense that I am not fully certain of, these heaps are also constitutive *levels* of being.

(1) The first heap or stage, and basic ingredient or fundamental level of a new being, is " The aggregate stream of the immately past life which descends to rebirth in a womb" at the moment of conception. It is comprised of ignorance (of its former births and its own

illusory nature), desire, grasping tendencies toward new life, and "mental impulsions of becoming." These comprise the basic karmic deposit from the past, as yet only potential but reaching out hungrily for new form. "The bulk of kamma is condensed into the first heap; the other three heaps preserve only the residue. For it is the first heap that is to be built into the parami self."

(2) The second heap, stage, stream, or level of personal being, is the receptacle-vehicle comprising the empirically perceivable "substance," as it were, of the five-fold body-mind individuality which each one of us is. It comes into being as a result of the combination of the first-heap karmic thrust or stream with the male and female physical elements. The thrusting-desiring-grasping impulse of the first stream draws to itself the as-yet-dissociated second-heap elements of new being, as a magnet attracts iron filings. The elements of this new five-fold being at first are "purely receptive and negative, and at birth are devoid of immediate ethical responsibility."

(3) The third heap, stream, or level, represents the past karmic inheritance of the first heap or stream, having received its renewed actual embodiment in the second-heap elements; and "it is this third stream which accumulates fresh kamma [karma] and condenses it down into the two preceding streams, leaving an impress therein." In other words, this third stage or stream of becoming is the new "self" *in active engagement with its environment in thought and action,* taking into itself at its deepest levels abiding influences and characteristics which will thenceforth be components of its essential nature. This is the dynamic-positive aspect of the new sentient being, in qualifying, altering, and interactive relation to what has been given it by karmic inheritance and to its new mind-body form (i.e. the sum of the first two streams). These two first streams, interacting with the individual's environment, form the enlarging, karma-accumulating individuality of the third heap, and comprise the ongoing base of personal process.

III

(4) From the third stream or heap or stage, as active and dynamic, arises the fourth one which is "futuristic in content. That is, a negative group for future rebirth and reception of impressions." This stage, or this stream, in confluence with the other streams and resulting from the other stages, represents the total "self" of successive states interacting externally with environment, internally with its own component streams, and all together thrusting forward in time by futuristic intention, thus accumulating a new karmic destiny.[1]

Now whether or not we grasp all the subtleties of this analysis, it is clear that it emphasizes in a second way the non-integrality of personal being, by portraying it as a bundle of streams or levels of energy-for-becoming, neither more nor less. But it brings into play another factor which represents the second perspective from which we can view the process of selfhood, namely the *longitudinal-section* view which calls attention to the factors of *continuity*. Now this *continuity*, even if not continuing *identity*, of successive states or stages of becoming, is fully as important as the non-integrality (according to the cross-sectional view) of the becoming-process (or person) at a given moment *For it is their continuity that gives the successive states their significance.* And that continuity, within the individual life stream is *absolutely integral*, with no mingling side-streams, no confluence of separate personal-being streams with each other. There may be a slight porosity of the banks of that stream of being that is I—that is, "outside" influences may penetrate my consciousness and influence my course—but the central identity of the forward thrust into new being, moment by moment, life by life, is purely my own; and this, not in the sense of an identical soul or self that passes from life to life, but in the sense of a self-contained Karmic stream of forward-thrusting-into-being, whose new states or positions in time are the result of one and only one linear set of previous body-mind events. To repeat: The karmic integrity of this individualized stream of being is absolute through the ages.

Now it is important for our purposes here to observe briefly the ideal perfection of the factor of *continuity* as achieved in the lives of the saints and Buddhas. They are initially subject to karma as other men, and are composed of the same four-heap and five-

IV

factor selfhood. But theirs is a superior use of karma. *For they are the embodiment of a victorious and ever-cumulative will-to-perfection.* Whereas the lives of ordinary beings describe an indecisive see-saw of varying karmic fortune and uncertain will, those who become saints and Buddhas do so by the unceasing performance of worthy and insightful deeds which cumulatively bear their fruit in an increased capacity for spiritual accomplishment and self-control that finally achieves a superior kind of cohesiveness. One may say that with such persons, the longitudinally-viewed cumulative continuity of their will-to-liberation becomes dominant over the cross-sectional quality of individuality as *anatta,* or " amorphous plurality." The forward-upward tending dynamism of this will-to-perfection is the *essential* quality of their karmic life-stream; they represent self-created centers of dynamic power for good. The mere blind thrust of Karmic energy into a new existence is progressively transformed into a fully conscious, deliberate and irresistible drive toward the perfection of enlightenment.

In passing, it may be observed that the only difference between the saint and the Buddha is the relative thickness, so to speak, of the sheaf of capacities composing this dynamic new self which each carries on into the future. *Sainthood* (as seen in Theravada Buddhism) is composed of a sheerly individualized will-to-release of the thickness of a needle-pointed thrust toward Nirvana. Buddhas, because of a million-fold number of existences lived under the compulsion of a vow to achieve ultimate Buddhahood, are by contrast massive forward thrusts of moral-mental perfections *(paramis)* which enable them, upon their final enlightenment, to teach and sustain others in the way to Nirvana, besides achieving their own Nirvana. And such is the force of these accumulated perfections that they somehow remain as a mystical and dynamically present force in the world *after* the Buddha has entered into his own inaccessible Nirvana.

II. Split-Personality Karma and its Cure

We are now ready to turn to the split-personality doctrine proposed by Mr. Magness. This doctrine may be stated thus: The loose congeries of factors that make up the pseudo-self of the cross-sectional view *(anatta* or non-self stream of being) may become

V

dissociated into new selves, especially upon death, each of which splinter selves or psychic-offshoots then takes its own separate course of karmic being—though it takes some time for such a self to accumulate much self-being even of the illusory sort. (It may wander as a disembodied spirit for long ages) In such an interpretation of *The Three Faces of Eve*, had Eve died when the three selves within her were struggling for mastery, she might have split into three new subselves who might not have recognized each other at their next encounter in their next lives. A quotation or two will give Mr. Magness' account of this situation:

"At death, due to lack of integration and purifcation at one firmly poised and oriented center, these four heaps of personality make a total split and go their ways."[2] (See Diagram I)

" When a man dies, the main stream of consciousness, or life-continuum process (bhavanga-sota), though it continues to activate as a stream, has offshoots. That is, under the force of the grasping impulsions which accumulated from antecedent environmental contact (but constrained by the centripetal gravitational force in the organism) the main stream is split off into substreams, each instinct with a separate life-continuum process of its own henceforth (not unlike the divided amoebae).

Thus, what it perpetuated is not static identical singularity but, rather amorphous plurality. Each separate life-continuum process is then propelled to its own kammic [karmic] destiny, sometimes taking rebirth immediately. Once separated thus, it would scarcely be to the point to say that one such life-continuum has any identification with another. The logical conclusion is that a man may meet one of his former life-continuum fragments incarnate and never so much as recognize the connection."[3]

VI

DIAGRAM I

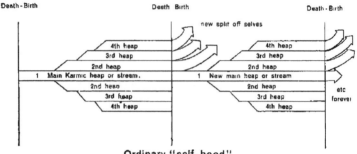

Ordinary "self-hood"
(Longitudinal section)

Here then is a variant form of the *anatta* or four-stream conception of being. It emphatically asserts that there is no true self-identical person at any moment, nor any identity carrying on from life; that dependent-origination-identity is not true identity. Yet it is different from the assertion that the five factors simply come apart upon death, in its statement that the pseudo-self comes apart into subordinate *selves*, or split-karmic streams—each of which becomes a new five-factor pseudo-self. For Mr. Magness this neatly explains or confirms two tangential Buddhist doctrines: (1) the seemingly infinite perpetuation of the number of selves to be reborn, though the "original" total number has been reduced by those attaining Nirvana; and (2) why it is that the memory of one's past lives attainable by psychic discipline peters out in the far past into an indistinct haze. The unperceivable beginning of a "self" represents its split-off point into sub-selfhood at some past time. Of course each splinter-self, though "but a recent product of environmental friction and contact," containing only a fraction of the parent stream's qualities, nevertheless as a proud pseudo-self "considers itself to be unique, god-given and eternal."[4]

Such is the negative side of psychic off-shoots, so to speak. Must one then consign himself to be thus forever split and re-split into an infinitude of sub-selves? most distressing to *self*-respecting Westerners! Where in all this is the hope of Nirvana? for Nirvana for all its seeming negativity is not a mere zero-end of self-fragmentation, but the maximization of one special sort of *self-becoming*. *The whole point of Mr. Magness' work is the delineation of the positive prospect of achieving "true self-integration,"* though this phrase is distinctly not Theravadin:

VII

"Thus also it is said that insofar as the individual is concerned he can be said to endure from existence to existence *only to the extent that his paramis* (perfect qualities of consciousness) *are preserved intact...*"[5]

"The way to release, therefore, is a unification, integration, and purging of all rebirth factors, so as to eliminate any further reproduction of the amorphous plurality which perpetuates existence in the world spheres, without end."[6]

The way of release is then a genuine integration of those factors found in the ongoing stream of pseudo-selfhood, which is only a series of successive states, causally related to each other but otherwise discontinuous, into a new self of genuine integrity, a self capable of salvation in Nirvana. It should be noted that this is the maximization of the element of continuity, observable in the longitudinal-section view of life and which is best achieved by the saints' and Buddhas' will-to-perfection. It is the creation, along the way, of a non-splitting, true selfhood composed of an enduring entity of spiritual deeds. (See Diagram II)

DIAGRAM II

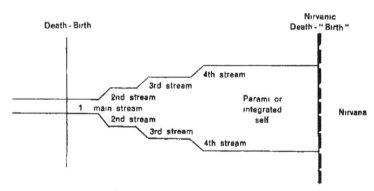

Achievement of an integrated
or "salvation-self"
(Longitudinal Section)

VIII

Before speaking a little further of the *religious* implications of this new and integral salvation-self, it is of interest to observe Mr. Magness' interpretation of the psychological process involved in the creation of this new self. Briefly, it is a process by which there is deliberately formed an integrated self-consciousness which is superior to, i.e. more deeply central and more tightly unified than, all of the separative self-fragments which compose ordinary and peripheral selves. It is a process in which all levels of the self are united into an integral unity; from the ongoing sub-conscious life-stream *(bhavanga-sota)* which flows onward even during sleep and is the lowest common denominator of all life, up to and including the highest levels of explicit consciousness of saintly and Buddha awareness. In response to my question as to whether some of his descriptions of the action and interaction of consciousness and subconsciousness during the process of self-remaking were Freudian or reverse-Freudian, Mr. Magness replied in part:

"The collective experience of the parami-self cannot be to the fore of consciousness in its completeness at any given moment. What is not to the fore is sunk and collected in a receptacle which is the bhavanga, its subconscious otherness... When it is said that the peripheral mind must be sunk down into the bhavanga, what is actually meant is to sink it down and then edge it up two fingerbreadths above the bhavanga... If it is not edged up, there will be no full awareness, there will be only submergence into the ceaseless random flow of the subconscious stream. It is edged up thus so as to be near the bhavanga stream, so that it can dip into it at will, just as one dips into a stream and retrieves flowing objects therein. It is correct to say that by so doing the peripheral mind is deepened and made aware of experiences unplumbed before (brought over from other lives, as well as opening new horizons which may arise). It is also correct to say that it is the redemption of the subconscious by making it conscious."[7]

Now some of the imagery here is esoterically Buddhist. The two-finger distance above the bhavanga-stream center, located near the navel, goes back to an ancient Hindu-Buddhist theory of psycho-physiology and its appropriate meditative techniques; nor is the picking up of the memories of past lives particulary Freudian no matter how vast the sub-conscious realm is conceived to be! But the psychological bearings are clear. Conscious and subconscious levels of awareness are broken open to each other, and by their interrelation a new integral unity is created, containing elements of both. Not only is the superficial ordinary consciousness brought into vital contact with its own inward roots and hidden sources, but the turbid irrational currents of the sub-conscious life-force (or Id) are brought to clarity, redeemed by consciousness, and made part of a new self-consciousness which is neither sub- nor super-but integral. As Mr. Magness goes on to say:

> "Because his subconscious is pure the arahatta [i.e. the saint ready for Nirvana] has no delusive or morbid dreams."[8]

But of course for the Buddhist the result is far more that the merely psychological renewal and integration of the person. It is a salvational process as well. This new self that results from the intermingling of the *bhavanga-sota* (subconscious continuum) and rational consciousness under proper auspices, is the parami-self. Its unification and purification of the ordinary fractionated pseudo-self's impulses and drives, constitutes a self capable of liberation from the *im*personality of karmic being, and preserves it unto true Nibbanic selfhood with no further fractioning.

As a consistent Buddhist, Mr. Magness is very emphatic that this new self is not the Hindu atman or primordial transcendent soul in disguise:

> "The nature of the transcendence of the new self that arises... is not to be considered as inherent in individuality, for that would be tantamount to championing the doctrine of a permanent soul flowing on unchanged, from some primordial source. It is indeed created by self-action, but by no means is the self which created it originally transcendent. It is not a matter of original transcendence but transmutation."[9]

And every human self has at least a latent capacity to thus take the elements of its *anatta* (non-or pseudo-self) and transmute them into a *finally* transcendent self.

X

Now does this integration or transmutation of self, which results in Nirvana's attainment, signify the utter cessation of selfhood? Mr. Magness quite emphatically denies such a conclusion. For, were annihilation the case:

> "It would be a contradiction in terms, for one does not integrate oneself through a process of aeons merely to disintegrate again into some ocean of forgetfulness. Super - selfhood [my phrase] is just the end - result of the aeonic process, and Buddhas at the moment in Nibbana [Nirvana] are certainly embued with consciousness or they wouldn't be what they are. Their radiance fills the ocean of Nibbana."[10]

III. Postscript

What is the significance of this doctrinal statement of Mr. Magness? Writes he: "I have proposed nothing new at all, but rather these doctrines have been imposed on me as the result of prolonged investigation. It is not book - learning which clarifies doctrines but the understanding which one brings thereto, revealing old doctrines in fresh light."[11] Nor is he concerned with whether "Buddhist orthodoxy" finds him "heretical" or not—since that "orthodoxy" is a body of inconsistent doctrinal variations, in his opinion.

At present I have only the view of one member of that orthodoxy, the Venerable Nyanaponika of Ceylon who, on the basis of a very short quotation from Mr. Magness' writes:

> "Therefore I agree with your correspondent that 'various of the component elements in a given human personality may split off into an independent existence and karmic career'—though I do not favour very much that rather coarse metaphor of "splitting off."[12]

To me also, as an outsider, Mr. Magness' doctrine seems to have considerable Buddhist logic about it and to make more rational the doctrine of the karmic inheritance of personal characteristics. For I quite agree with him when he writes: "It is always wrong in Buddhist circles to reduce everything to a naked karma-thrust."[13]

To me it also seems that Mr. Magness has courageously made explicit what is largely implicit and subdued, and somewhat illogical, in Theravada orthodoxy because of its deep addiction to negative language, namely, the *dynamically positive quality of Buddhist salvation as a process of building a higher, more integrated self.* (For "self" is always an evil term in Theravada no-soul orthodoxy.) But actually "self-building" has a significant parallel in the widely received Theravada presumption that the infinite store of the Buddha's accumulated merits (*his parami* self) remains as a *presently available and dynamic force for good and salvation among men,* though the Buddha himself, as an empirically perceptible self, has passed on into theoretically inaccessible Nirvana. And as I see it, the forging of an enduring *parami*-self, wrought of good deeds done in a meditational wisdom - context, is the *essence* of saint - making or salvation in Buddhism. It is therefore Mr. Magness' great importance to attempt to rescue the anatta (no-self) doctrine from its sheer negativity; and the conception of karmic thrust from its sheerly naked characterless propulsion into new being.[14] And it is of great interest, and perhaps significance, that this no doubt represents a manifestation of the new *experiential* emphasis in Theravada Buddhism, consequent upon the layman's very recent venture into the former exclusively monkish preserve of meditational discipline.

XII

FOOTNOTES

1. All quotations from letter of July 13, 1963.
2. Letter, July 13, 1963.
3. *Samma Ditthi*, p. 69.
4. *Samma Ditthi*, p. 72.
5. *Ibid*, p. 69 (Italics added).
6. *Ibid*, p. 70
7. Letter, July 13, 1963, p. 1.
8. Letter, July 13, 1963.
9. Letter, July 13, 1963, p. 2.
10. Letter, July 13, 1963, p. 1.
11. Letter of September 15, 1963.
12. Letter of July 3, 1963.
13. Letter of note 9.
14. Part of the "characterlessness" of the Karmic thrust into new being may arise from my own misinterpretation of Buddhist Karma. In any case I had not been so sharply aware, before reading Mr. Magness' writings, of other alternatives to the seeming bareness (i.e. devoidness of personal qualities) of the Karmic thrust of one life into new individuality.

THE DHAMMAKAYA

(Metaphysical Implications)

THE DHAMMAKAYA
(Metaphysical Implications)

In the Agganna Sutta of the Digha Nikaya it is said:
Tathagatassa h'etam Vasettha adhivacanam Dhammakayo iti pi...
That is. Vasettha, Dhammakaya is the designation by which the Tathagata is genuinely known.

This declaration, seemingly so simple, has been interpreted to imply that the body of teaching left by the Buddha is being referred to. How such a conclusion is arrived at is a mystery and requires a large stretch of the imagination. In fact, the implications underlying this utterance can be comprehended only by those who practice the highest scale of concentrated jhana. This, though clearly implied in the Dhammasangani of the Abhidhamma, is seldom grasped. Herein it is said:

The aspirant (yogavacara puggala) develops the four foundations of mindfulness (satipatthana) to supramundane status, develops the four great efforts (samappadhana)...the four supernormal qualities (iddhipada)...the five potential faculties (indriya) ...the five powers (bala)... the seven factors of enlightenment (sambojjanga). the four truths (sacca)... the quality of tranquillity (samatha)... the factors of existence (dhamma)... the fivefold personality group (khandha)... the eighteen elements (dhatu).. the nutritive essences (ahara) .. contact (phassa)... feeling (vedana) .. perception (sanna)... volition (cetana)... mind (citta) to supramundane status. Which is the centripetal force which projects the aspirant out of this world to release, leaving false views and the rest behind, attaining the streamenterer (sotapanna) stage, the once·returner (sakadagamin) stage, the non-returner (anagamin) stage, and the emancipated (arahatta) stage, respectively .. free from sensuality, free from blemish, accompanied by reasoning and reflection, bliss and well-being, born of solitude and dispassion. attaining the first jhana, the second, the third, the fourth, the fifth jhana (lokuttara).

1

Although this is easy to repeat it is seldom understood and even less accomplished. Nevertheless, it is here that the technique by which the Dhammakaya is attained is laid forth. That is, the technique of transubstantiation, of transmuting mundane factors (commencing with mindfulness up to contact and the rest) to their supramundane limit and counterparts. The transformation of the five-fold personality base, the elements of personality, contact, feeling, perception, volition and mentality from the status of the fettered worldling to the emancipated group (khandha vimutto). This is achieved by the jhanic factor of concentration, of an intensification process. Which stated in Abhidhammic terms (magga citta vithi) goes as follows:

  (1) Bhavanga calana (vibrating passivity of subconsciousness)

  (2) Bhavanga upaccheda (passive arrestation of subconsciousness)

  (3) Manodvaravajjana (mind-door receptivity)

  (4) Parikamma javana (initial impulsion)

  (5) Upacara javana (access concentration impulsion)

  (6) Anuloma javana (directed-process impulsion)

  (7) Gotrabhu javana (change-of-lineage impulsion)

  (8) Sotapanna Magga javana (Stream-enterer Path impulsion)

  (9) Sotapanna Phala javana (Stream-enterer Fruition impulsion)

  (10) Sotapanna Phala javana 2 (Stream-enterer Fruition 2).

  (11) Bhavanga (subconsciousness)

This is the transmutative refining process of mental concentration in action. That is, before this the Sotapanna consciousness did not exist, but now through the process of jhanic intensification and direction it has come into existence, and shall continue to so exist as a resultant (vipaka) level henceforth in the bhavanga base. From which base it has to be edged up to concentrated pitch again if the intention is to process it a step higher on the path, which is as follows:

2

(1) Bhavanga calana
(2) Bhavanga upaccheda
(3) Manodvaravajjana
(4) Parikamma javana (this can be dispensed with in the adept)
(5) Upacara javana
(6) Anuloma javana
(7) Gotrabhu javana
(8) Sakadagamin Magga javana
(9) Sakadagamin Phala javana
(10) Sakadagamin Phala javana 2
(11) Bhavanga...

And so on for the Anagamin and Arahatta stages, respectively.

From this may be gleaned the wide implications of Buddha's statement that all things arise from causes and conditions. There is no eternalism (it didn't exist before) nor annihilationism (it is not destroyed) involved, but that when this arises that arises through succession of cause and effect, and that when this disappears that disappears too. If there is a cause (hetu) an effect (vipaka) appears, and for a path (magga) a fruition (phala). This is in essence the structure whereby mentality and physicality as parallel processes function in the world of personality as well as in the larger scope of impersonal universality.

Insofar as the Dhammakaya is concerned, it commences and takes form at the Gotrabhu impulsion instant, and on up to the Sotapanna etc. Thus there is the Dhammakaya Gotrabhu, the Dhammakaya Sotapanna, the Dhammakaya Sakadagamin, the Dhammakaya Anagamin, the Dhammakaya Arahatta. All these Dhammakaya forms are capable of still higher refinement and may be replicated at will;

The Dhammakaya is a composite impermeation and fusion of element and essence (dhatu - dhamma). That is, commencing from the normal fivefold field of personality, element and essence aggregates are pushed (bhavana) into the path (of morality, concentration, and intelligence) until they change their lineage (from mundane to supramundane) to emerge (phala as release aggregates (khandha vimutto). The specific field of personality is still

3

there, only its *quality* has been changed, transmuted and transformed. It is no longer mundane, it has become supramundane. One impulsion has become objectified in another, one actuality transmuted into the next, until their most translucent qualities have emerged. This is the perfection of consciousness through the right technique of intensification and the attainment of the higher mind (adhicitta). It is this transcendent mind, purged of mundane residues, which the emancipated ones take with him (as a bird its wings) in final withdrawal. In view of its being a 'release' (vimutti) form and vehicle, this Dhammakaya cannot be said to have previously existed or not. Not comprehending the implications of the intensifications of the Dhammakaya process, it is only natural that the following declaration of the Buddha remains a mystery and is so often confused as to be interpreted into mere meaningless negativity :

"Since in this very life a Tathagata is not to be regarded as existing, is it proper to speak of him thus: the Tathagata comes to be after death, he comes not to be after death, he both comes to be and comes not to be after death, he neither comes to be nor comes not to be after death... A Tathagata released from what is called mundane form, feeling, perception, aggregates and consciousness is profound, immeasurable, hard to plumb, like the great ocean. It is not fitting to state that he is reborn, not reborn, both reborn and not reborn, neither reborn nor not reborn."

In view of the fact that even in this very life the Dhammakaya of the Buddha remains unperceived, whether the aggregates of the human form are present or not makes no difference at all, and the terms life and death therefore do not apply. Due to lack of insight, the layman labours under the misconception that release is a state bordering on extinction, arriving at this view through inference, with the Buddha word itself as reference : neither reborn etc. However, what follows is a refutation :

"A Tathagata is to be proclaimed in *other* than these four ways."

To comprehend this it is necessary to penetrate into the processes of causality. Only through right insight into causal processes will the bits of the big jigsaw puzzle that is the dhamma fall into place. Otherwise nothing but confusion will arise, unable to come to terms :

4

"The world, Kaccayana, is for the most part attached to two extremes... Transcending these extremes (eternalism and annihilationism) the Tathagata (through right insight) expounds dhamma by way of cause."

As usual, it is from the human plane that a launching pad has to be made. This is so because:

"Man's eye, ear, nose, tongue, body, and mind, are as an ocean. Their motion is made up of shapes, of sounds, of smells, of tastes, of sensations, of ideas. He who conquers these stands upon the other shore. One who has reached the other shore, O Bhikkhus, thinks thus: this raft has been of great use to me, resting on it I have crossed to the further shore. Suppose now I haul it up or sink it down into the deep and go my ways By so doing, O Bhikkhus, that man would have finished with the raft."

The sixfold field of contact is always at the root of knowledge. It is to be observed that among the concomitants of consciousness (cetasikas), contact (phassa) comes first, followed by feeling (vedana), perception (sanna), volition (cetana), concentration (ekaggata), vitality (jivitindriya), and attention (manasikara). As these seven factors are common to all forms of consciousness and are always present therein as it flows along its haphazard way, why does the above statement seem to depreciate the field of sense-contact? If individuality is not the creation of an Overlord, but self - creation through a long and tedious assimilation process, a process of assimilating potential resources into the orbit of one common centre, why has it to be abandoned even as a raft?

There is no contradiction here if it is realized that even after the raft is finished with, the *person* who crossed thereon remains And if the person remains, then the field of contact also remains, and what is left aside is only the vehicle of transport Namely, the mundane husk of personality The confusion has always been to annihilate the person together with the raft. Little is it taken into consideration that the development of emancipation as a definite end - result necessitates the presence of a mind which achieves the emancipation. Although the mind and the self may be reduced to a series of occasions of contact, the totality of the occasions of contact stemming down the stream of consciousness from life to life, this does not preclude that the collective nuclei of cognition once arisen must perish. They are recorded in the subconscious stream (bhavanga) as the stuff of life, impressed therein. They only disappear from perceptive immediacy, but they can be recalled by the right technique.

When Buddha classified the factors of existence (dhamma) under ten heads, he began with the statement that the root of dhamma is will (cetana), that dhamma arises whensoever attention (manasikara) is focussed thereon, that dhamma appears through contact (phassa), and is combined with the aid of perception (sanna). This is only in keeping with the functions of process, and that for psychic emancipation as an end - result (all dhammas have release as goal) to culminate necessitates duration in time. Further, when the psyche attains its maturity even as a fruit, it is in deathlessness submerged. However, as it begins its character the only food it knows is contact: for consciousness arises by way of occasion and without occasion there can be no arising thereof. The occasion (of contact) can be either internal (ajjhata) or external (bahiddha) as the case may be, and its character may be either wholesome (kusala) or the reverse (akusala) dependent on the circumstances in which it takes its rise, being, so to speak, perfumed thereby.

Although all in life is mutation, the mutation itself proceeds along certain lines, and insofar as individuality is concerned, in separate streams. In that life proceeds along separate streams makes it possible for the quality of mindfulness (sati) to exist. In fact, it is in proportion to the quantity of mindfulness in any given stream of individual life which determines it as an orientation point and centre of selfhood. The stream of consciousness without mindfulness is only made too evident in nightmares, or daymares, as the case may be. Among the seven factors of the enlightened mind mindfulness comes first, for it is the rock on which enlightenment stands. Once mindfulness is established as a point of orientating selfhood, investigation of things (dhamma vicaya) follows, and detailed analysis. This again entails effort (viriya). But since effort by itself tends to agitation, it is regulated by the factors of bliss (piti), calm (passadhi). concentration (samadhi), and equanimity (upekkha). These complete the seven limbs of wisdom (satta sambojjanga), so called.

With the aid of these limbs, the mind perceives passion and purges itself thereof. Perceives hatred, delusion, lethargy, distrac-

6

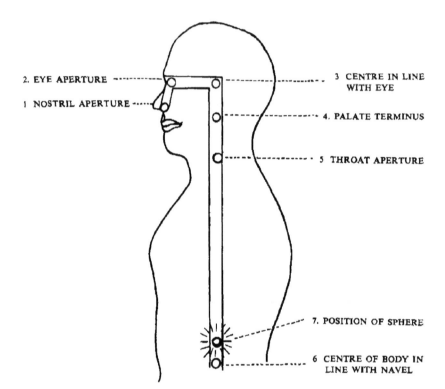

2. EYE APERTURE

1 NOSTRIL APERTURE

3 CENTRE IN LINE WITH EYE

4. PALATE TERMINUS

5 THROAT APERTURE

7. POSITION OF SPHERE

6 CENTRE OF BODY IN LINE WITH NAVEL

THE SPHERE AT THE CENTRE OF THE BODY IN RELATION
TO THE ELEMENTS

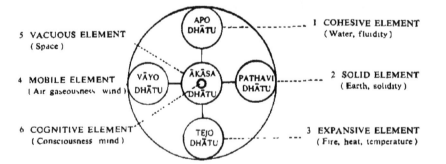

5 VACUOUS ELEMENT
(Space)

4 MOBILE ELEMENT
(Air gaseousness wind)

6 COGNITIVE ELEMENT
(Consciousness mind)

APO DHĀTU

VĀYO DHĀTU

ĀKĀSA DHĀTU

PATHAVI DHĀTU

TEJO DHĀTU

1 COHESIVE ELEMENT
(Water, fluidity)

2 SOLID ELEMENT
(Earth, solidity)

3 EXPANSIVE ELEMENT
(Fire, heat, temperature)

tion, and purges itself thereof. Perceives the undeveloped mind, and develops it. Perceives the superior mind and develops it. Perceives the mind with nothing higher than it, and remains firm therein. Perceives the mind as firm, perceives the mind as emancipated, and remains emancipated.

This is one aspect. The mind imbued with mindfulness perceives forms in forms, feelings in feelings, consciousness in consciousness, intangibles in intangibles. Perceives form, feeling, perception, impressions, and consciousness arising and vanishing from moment to moment. Perceives the internal sixfold base of cognition and the sixfold external base, and how through the interaction of these the mind is fettered and becomes subject to their sway. Perceives suffering, its origin, its dissipation, and the way thereto. The mind perceiving this remains calm, detached, clinging to nothing in the world. It perceives its own arising in perceptive immediacy. Immediacy, that is, by moment, by continuity, and by delimitation of the subject field.

Now the point of orientation where mindfulness is established by those who would aspire to the highest pitch of insight is at the pit of the diaphragm, just two finger-breadths above the navel line (See Diagram). There is a deliberate sinking of the peripheral faculties right down into the centre of the hollow space element (akasadhatu). In this hollow space element the cognitive element must sink, where by concentration (bhavana) it is smelted down and purged, whence it brightens and begins to glow. This is the implication of Buddha's advice to his own son:

"Both the personal and external elements are to be regarded as they really are, by perfect insight: this is not mine, not this am I, herein is not the self of me. So regarding them, one is repelled by them and cleanses one's heart thereof."

That is, commencing from this preliminary technique of introverting the faculties to basic centre, concentration is intensified and pushed down into the void receptacle (natthi paccaya) so that under its impression a refined replica of it emerges with all its formations complete:

"It also has a form and is made of mind, complete in all its limbs, possesed of super sense organs. That is the mind-made self."

7

If this is difficult to understand it need only be mentioned that each moment of contact (phassa) is a creative force, a replicative process, a subjective - objective flux, of reciprocity, which is the stuff of life. Nature (dhamma) contains the possibility of an infinite refinement in its processes, and mind - made selves are only the life principle being processed by the appropriate technique, which culminates in the formation of the Dhammakaya. For which formation a great introversion has to be made, of bending the mind down to deep centre to witness things in their true perspective:

"Thus steadied, perfectly purified and translucent, free from blemish, purged of taint, made supple and pliable, fit for wielding, established and immovable, I *bent down* my mind to the recalling of my former existences..."

In each form which proceeds from the human base, right up to the Dhammakaya Arahatta, there is feeling, consciousness, and mental essences in ever ascending scale of refinement, in emergent style. It is this process which the Satipatthana Sutta would have us observe in detail:

"Thus he lives contemplating form internally... origination factors, or dissolution factors, or both... Thus he contemplates form in form, feeling in feeling, consciousness in consciousness, and mental essence in mental essence"

The central core of the ideal, therefore, in no way signifies annihilation of the life - process (jivitindriya) but a development and cultivation process, to the refinedest degrees. Thus, the Dhammakaya, like all other forms, is itself possessed of feeling, perception, impressions, and consciousness. This is pure groupage (visuddhi khandha), or the release group (khandha vimutto). It is to be understood that the purity pristine of the emancipated one in no way precludes that the said consciousness must necessarily be devoid of sense - impressions or character. It only implies that the emancipated one has ceased to grasp at them as his 'self', and being unattached thereby, has transmuted himself into the realities of pure form, together with the insight and vision into another dimension.

Dhamma is both abstract and concrete: it arises through environmental contact, traversed in spatio - temporal fact, through the right technique becomes transcendent, and finally outlives its mundane base, leaving it behind. They, the mundane bases, are left behind because they are the factors which grasp (upadana-khandha) at contacts and send life reeling into pain, with all manner of psychic offshoots, the split-process of personality which is the origin of amorphous plurality (anatta). By leaving these behind, suffering is reduced to zero, consciousness brought to highest pitch.

In the last analysis, everything rests on the statement: attahi attano natho...

That is: Self is the refuge of self. And, again: attadipa attasarana nannassarana, dhammadipa dhammasarana nannassa-rana. Self is the isle, self the refuge, no other refuge is there. Dhamma is the isle, dhamma the refuge, no other refuge is there.

How the self—in a world of no-self—is the isle and refuge can be grasped only in terms of a fixed orienting point of consciousness. There is no need to look elsewhere for any self, because the orienting point has to be established by a deep retreat within. To push on in until 'a vortex of energy' grips the mind, so that which is not yet won might be won, by human strength, by human striving. This is so because the root of dhamma is will, and dhamma arises whensoever attention is focussed on it, brought to be by contact, combined by perception, and culminated by jhanic equipoise.

The isle and the refuge referred to is nothing other than the sphere of dhamma to be processed at the diaphragm pit two finger breadths above the navel. To be processed at this integral point until complete integration is established and the split-personality of anatta becomes the self-sufficient base of atta. Thus will the limit of darkness be reached. For this, it cannot be too often repeated that a process of profound involution has to be achieved, purging the mind of what it is not. As Lao Tze observes:

"The excellence of a dwelling is its site. The excellence of a mind is its profundity."

Penetration by the involuted technique mentioned sinks consciousness deeper and deeper into dhamma which is supra-mundane and, as a consequence, accomplishes ascendancy over external supports and mundane spatiality. The spatiality which presents itself to the five sense-door field of apprehension upholds the four basic principles of elemental solidity, cohesive liquidity, temperature, and atmospheric pressure. Pure space, uncompounded and underived, exists in primal state as the unconditioned (nibbanadhatu) element, or, as it is called, the unformed (asankhata dhatu). Which is cognized only by the purified mind (vinnanam) of the Dhammakaya.

Although the practice of submerging the peripheral faculties by the involuted technique is difficult of assay at first, it can be achieved. In fact, it is already a normal course of nature for the faculties to sink to the diaphragm position whenever sleep descends, otherwise sleep would never ensue. Sleepless nights are passed due to this refusal of the peripheral faculties to sink down from the brain to bhavanga substrate, which is their home base. For even as a man steps out of home each morn, to return at dusk, even so the human consciousness, as much as it may wander out when awake, in sleep returns to base, its natural resting place.

With the refinement of the conscious field, extra-sensory perception is developed For the difficulties which beset the beginner who strives for such vision, the Upakkilesa Sutta, Sunnata Vagga, of the Majjhima Nikaya, gives us a glimpse. It is related how Buddha while residing at Kosambi was approached by three bhikkhus headed by Anuruddha who requested him to explain why whilst practicing meditation they were unable to attain supernormal vision for long.

"Anuruddha, even I in the period before my enlightenment, not yet enlightened, still a bodhisatta, I too saw light (supernormal) and forms, but not for long. What, thought I, was the cause and condition for this?

"At which the knowledge arose in me that defilements (upakkilesa) were the condition and cause. Namely, doubt (vicikiccha), lack of attention (amanasikara), sloth and torpor (thina middha), fear (chambhitatta), excitement (ubbilla), impurity of mind (dutthulla), excess of zeal (accaraddha viriya), lack of zeal (atilina viriya), desire (abhijappa), restlessness of mind (nanatta sanna), over fixation on an object or objects of mind (atinijjhayitatta).

10

"Anuruddha, whensoever either one of these eleven defilements arose in me, my concentration was shaken, that defilement being its cause. Whensoever my concentration was shaken, light and forms also vanished. Therefore I strove to discover the method whereby these defilements could be removed, and did accordingly. Knowing doubt and the rest as defilements of consciousness, I removed them from my mind.

"Anuruddha, not unheedless, with vigour, I concentrated my mind. Sometimes I saw light but no forms. Other times I saw forms but no light During the night, during the day, both night and day. At which doubt arose in me. What was the cause, the condition, for this?

"Anuruddha, I thought to myself, at such a time as I thought not of forms, thought only of light, at such a time I saw only light, saw no forms. At such a time as I thought not of light, thought only of forms, at such a time I saw only forms, saw no light. During the night, during the day, both night and day.

"Anuruddha, not unheedless, with vigour, I concentrated my mind. Sometimes I saw only a little light, saw only a few forms. At other times I saw much light, saw many forms. During the night, during the day, both night and day. At which doubt arose in me. What was the cause, the condition, for this?

"Anuruddha, I thought to mspelf, at such a time when my concentration was lax, at such a time vision was lax. With vision lax as this, I therefore saw little light, saw only a few forms. At such a time when my concentration was great, at such a time vision was great. With vision great as this, I therefore saw much light, saw many forms. During the night, during the day, both night and day."

Again, when Buddha was once in Gayasisa, beside the river Gaya, he delivered the following address to a multitude of monks:

"Bhikkhus, in the period before my enlightenment, not yet enlightened, still a bodhisatta, while I was practicing concentration, I saw light, but saw no forms.

"Bhikkhus, the thought arose in me: if I were to see light as well as forms, this would be the attainment of extra - sensory perception (nanadassana) which is pure indeed. Therefore, in the period which ensued I, not unheedless, with vigour, with concentrated mind, saw forms. But failed to communicate with these.

"Bhikkhus, the thought arose in me: if I were not only to see light and forms, but were also to communicate with these, this would be the attainment of extra-sensory perception which is pure indeed. Therefore, in the period which ensued I, not unheedless, with vigour, with concentrated mind, saw light, saw forms, as well as communicated with these. But failed to discover from which astral group they came.

"Bhikkhus, the thought arose in me: if I were not only to see light... but were also to discover from which astral group they came, this would be the attainment of extra-sensory perception which is pure indeed. Therefore, in the period which ensued I... came to discover from which astral group they came. But failed to discover where, after having departed (cuti) from this life these astral forms again arose (uppatti) in rebirth, through whatever resultant force (kamma vipaka).

"Bhikkhus, the thought arose in me: if I were not only to see light... but were to discover where these astral forms arose in rebirth... were to discover on what food (ahara) they lived, suffered what pain or enjoyed what bliss, were of what age and lived for just how long... were to discover that I myself had lived or had not lived with them before... Therefore, in the period which ensued I, not unheedless... came to discover all of these.

"Bhikkhus, so long as my vision regarding these remained unclear, even so long in this world, deva world, brahma world, among ascetics and brahmins, gods and men, highest knowledge and insight (anuttara sammasambodhi nana) remained to be attained. But vision had arose in me: that my mind was free, this was my last birth, there was no more birth for me."

The process of attaining to a self-sufficient futurity is indeed (to borrow Whitehead's terminology): the process of eliciting into actual being factors in the universe which antecedently to that process exist only in the mode of unrealized potentialities. The process of self-creation is the transformation of the potential into the actual, and the fact of such transformation includes the immediacy of self-enjoyment... In the present, future occasions, as individual realities, with their measure of absolute completeness are non-existent. In the present there are no individual occasions belonging to the future. The present contains the utmost verge of such realized individuality. The whole doctrine of the future is to be understood in terms of the process of self-completion of each individual occasion.

That is, by contact (phassa), whether mental or physical. But as it is in the nature of processes, whether physical or mental, to perish and rearise with each moment, therefore perishing is the initiation of becoming, and how the past perishes is how the future becomes Aggregates of mentality (nama) serve as the base for the perpetuation of mentality by six conditions (paccaya). That is: continuity by momentum (anantara paccaya), direct contiguity of succession (samanantara paccaya), volitional impulsion (asevana paccaya), association factors (sampayutta paccaya), receptacle of voidness (natthi paccaya), and the quality of proceeding forth (vigata paccaya)

To be specific, in the process of establishing 'self as the refuge of self' by the jhanic method (the only method) the mind gradually withdraws from all contact with the body and concentrates itself by itself In the process, it encompasses itself with morality, because 'great becomes the fruit, great the advantage of concentration when it is encompassed by morality, and wisdom when encompassed by concentration, which wisdom sets the mind free'. These are signified by the spheres, or auras, of the said qualities of dhamma, which become developed in intensity as the process moves on to its highest pitch.

The whole process is one of greater and ever greater intensification of mind, with the understood implication that each antecedent moment of consciousness, with its set of ingrained qualities, through the very force of momentum (anantara paccaya) serves as the template or base for the production of a more refined conscious form, which again in turn serves as the base for the next, in ever refining chain reactive scale.

In this fashion, self becomes the refuge of self. No other profounder process is there, and in no profounder sense can it be understood. Indeed, with the expansion of the range of conscious-

13

ness, as it reaches its refinedest pitch, the self becomes an extremely extensive isle and refuge, so that no other refuge is elsewhere sought. This is the attainment of the Arahatta's self - sufficiency, moving wheresoever he pleases, taking with him nothing but his 'isle of self', even as a bird its wings.

Now as the peripheral faculties (of perception, memory, consciousness, and knowledge) sink right down into the diaphragm position and impermeate the areas of experience garnered from past lives (vipaka cittani), they become absorbed therein, and take on for the duration of that concentration the particular sphere of experience and refinement. Each stage of concentration has its specific nature, refined to scale, and, as a consequence, the plane of being and outlook is brought higher and higher as consciousness is winnowed away from the five human sense - door field of contact.

Thus, indeed, if whoever should practice depth concentration and witness in due order of refinement the emergence of form in form, feeling in feeling, consciousness in consciousness, mental essence in mental essence, originations and dissolutions, then the result is conclusive: being the only way which leads to the purification of creatures, to the destruction of grief and despair, to the attainment of the method, to the realization of Nibbana.

As dhamma arises whensoever attention is focussed on it, the more refined dhamma becomes the greater its range and scope becomes, until its field expands and embraces worlds and worlds. The human, the celestial, the brahma, the arupabrahma, and the Dhammakaya forms are archetypes of the psyche, and possess their characteristic feature and impress whereby they are recognized. Also, when they are attained, each bears the particular resemblance of the individulal who attains them. This is only in accordance with the principles of process, whereby a certain quantity when smelted down changes its form but still retains the elemental impress of which it is composed, the features with which it is stamped.

In the text of the Visuddhi Magga it is briefly stated how the forms are attained:

"Establish the human form in consciousness (of jhana) as hollow. It becomes hollow. Whence advert to another form

14

therein, and having done the preliminary work once more (of establishing it in consciousness of jhana as hollow) resolve that another form emerge therefrom. Then draw it out like a reed from its sheath... The sheath is one, the reed is another. But it was from the sheath that the reed was pulled. Even so the mind-made forms."

When it is said that the human form becomes hollow, it does so through the power of the jhanic will. At such moments, when the will is harnessed in any aim, results conform immediately to wish. Jhana achieves much which it is impossible for the normal consciousness to achieve. As the mind sinks back to the normal consciousness it requires the crude supports of the human plane. Food (ahara) is a basic necessity, but it may be dispensed with as long as jhana lasts, for the jhanic consciousness exists only on mental contact (phassa ahara), but crude food becomes inevitable with a return to human normalcy. Nevertheless, a distaste for crudity lingers on in the adept whose physical vitality has not completely reasserted itself, traces of jhanic absorption prevailing even after a return to the human plane.

All states of consciousness have the five aggregates of personality as base, only becoming more refined as they change their lineage from mundane to supramundane The fivefold aggregate evolves through the fourfold factors of kamma, antecedent consciousness, temperature, and nutriment. Kamma determines the destiny and disposal, for it is the initial authority which like a magnet draws to it the destiny to be wrought, dependent on antecedent aggregates. It determines the type of organism that is to issue forth and the consequent environment in which it is to evolve. But kamma itself is no rigid force. it may be deviated, take its effect in this life, the next, in a succession of lives, neutralized, weakened, substituted. There are causes and conditions for these fluctuations depending on shifts of what at a moment predominates, and what is subsidiary. As for consciousness which is reborn, it supplies the base from which name-and-form (nama-rupa) takes its rise. Temperature and nutriment support the name-and-form which then evolves, nourishing its physicality

When the five aggregates interpenetrate into an organic whole and absorb the environment, they are caught in the web of

15

its activity for good or ill. Whatever antecedent existence there was is forgotten, and since the immediate environment prevails consciousness is meshed therein, no chord of memory is evoked, until such time as jhanic attention is focussed on the past, or some sensory impression revivifies it to perceptive immediacy. However, unless intensified by jhanic technique, haphazard recollection of past lives by casual contact soon loses its impress because the connecting links are usually vague and because other immediate impressions whirl it away from sustained apprehension. Nevertheless, the character of past lives does play a significant part in the present, and in the case of sinners who become great saints especially so. That is, in the beginning before basic character can assert itself, the immediate environment meshes consciousness in its web of evil, but as time activates innate disposition to assert itself, a radical orientation takes place, brought about by pulsations (vinnatti) of significance, and what is called a 'conversion' is made. This is amply exemplified in the case of Angulimala the notorious bandit in Buddha's time.

Now when it is said in the scriptures that Buddha converts this one or that, that the 'spotless eye of the doctrine' arises in them. What does this imply? The fact that at that moment the Dhammakaya is perceived. It rises to the eye in a flash, with or without previous notice. It is, however, inadequate to state that there is no previous preparation, because these special ones have already accumulated the requisite potential in antecedent lives. Besides, at that moment Bubdha himself is controlling them, (psychically), though of course unknown and unseen by them.

However, although the Sotapanna stage and Sakadagamin stage may be attained in this way, they have still to be reborn, as their attainment is not complete. When they are reborn they too forget their past and go their ways as normal men of the world Until such time, of course, as when their peripheral faculties sinking, by concentration or by chance, perceive once more the Dhammakaya sphere arise For until complete integration in Arahattaship is attained the peripheral faculties are susceptible to anatta (split - personality), and even stream - enterers and once-returners produce offshoots of personality at death, the peripheral surplus of the immediate life removed.

When the consciousness (patisandhi vinnana) of a Sotapanna
or Sakadagamin is relinked in rebirth, it sinks to subconscious base
(bhavanga sota) at diphragm pit in the womb, completing its
functional cycle. For the cycle of a resultant entity (vipaka citta)
is only threefold: to depart (cuti), to relink in rebirth (patisandhi),
and to sink to subconsciousness (bhavanga). Although this subconscious quantity serves as the base for the arising of a fresh
name - and - form (nama - rupa), it is distinct therefrom. That is,
the resultant quantity remains a Sotapanna or a Sakadagamin, but
the fresh aggregates which arise develop into another personality
which at death splits off, the Sotapanna going one way and other
offshoots other ways. They bear away with them whatever
impressions (sankharas) are ingrained by attachment (upadana)
and the debris of their kammic heritage. The main stream of the
Sotapanna or Sakadagamin bears away the main draught of
kamma, leaving the dregs to the offshoots. Before these offshoots
can be Sotapannas themselves the cycle of revolution will have to
cover hundreds of kalpas before they too can attain the stream
This is so because the potential of a fresh entity is insufficient to
bear it up and experience the pitch of a semi - liberated suspense.

The offshoots of any given main stream never exceed three.
If the original continuum is counted, the series is in four. This
process of multiplication is to be deplored as the result of ignorance
(avijja) as its negative root, and desire (tanha) as its positive
cause. The offshoots vary in proportion to the conflicting impulses
which activate and divide personality into what it is, which bound
together by the organism are unable to set themselves free, but
which split apart at death, each possessing a separate existence
henceforth.

That there are twenty characteristics (akara) in four streams
or heaps (sankhepa) of personality, is to be analyzed in the light
of the formula of dependent origination (paticca samuppada).
Firstly, there is the aggregate stream of the last life which descends
to rebirth in a womb. This is a fivefold aggregate comprising of
ignorance (avijja), psychic data (sankharas), desire (tanha),
grasping (upadana), and becoming (bhava).

Secondly, we have the aggregate stream which, once the first
stream has fused in the womb, gives rise to another fivefold set

17

which is purely resultant in status. This is comprised of consciousness (vinnana), mentality and form (nama rupa), the six sense group (salayatana), contact (phassa), and feeling (vedana). Their status is purely receptive and negative, and at birth are devoid of immediate responsibility.

Thirdly, as environmental contact is established, another fivefold aggregate stream accumulates, whose function is immediate and positive. Comprising desire (tanha), grasping (upadana), becoming (bhava), ignorance (avijja), and psychic data (sankharas). It is this third stream which accumulates fresh kamma, and condenses it down into the two preceding streams, the preceding two being negative and ethically neutral insofar as this present life is concerned. However, their influence on this third stream is basic, as in the status of father to offspring.

Fourthly, the third stream serves as the base for the arising of another aggregate stream, comprising of consciousness (vinnana), mentality and form (nama rupa), the six sense group (salayatana), contact (phassa), and feeling (vedana).

At death, due to lack of sufficient integration, these four aggregate streams make a total split and go their ways.

It was the spectacle of this form of dependent origination on which Buddha concentrated (in direct order and inverse) at his enlightenment, witnessing in true perspective how life comes to be. Namely, that all life is without permanent identity (sabbe dhamma anattati), a flux of personalities, reciprocally based, originating anew from birth to birth.

These so-called split-personalities originate in the scope of 24 modes of conditionality (paccaya). And there are six groups thereof :

Firstly, mentality is the base for the arising of mentality (nama paccaya nama) by 6 modes. Namely, continuity by momentum (anantara paccaya), direct immediacy of contiguity (samanantara paccaya), volitional impulsion (asevana paccaya), association factors (sampayutta paccaya), receptacle of voidness (natthi paccaya), and the function of proceeding forth (vigata paccaya).

Secondly, mentality is the base for the arising of mentality-formations (nama paccaya namarupa) by 5 modes. Namely, root causality (hetu paccaya), concentrated absorption (jhana paccaya), path means (magga paccaya), immediate causality (kamma paccaya), and resultancy thereof (vipaka paccaya).

Thirdly, mentality is the base for the arising of formations (nama paccaya rupa) by 1 mode. Namely, consequence (paccajata paccaya). That is, it is the mentality aggregates which support the body, otherwise the body would not be able to continue as a living organism.

Fourthly, formations serve as the base for the arising of mentality (rupa paccaya nama) by 1 mode. Namely, antecedence (purejata paccaya). That is, it is what the body and its senses gather for it that makes the mentality aggregate continue to live in its environment and proceed.

Fifthly, mentality-formations serve as the base for the arising of mentality (pannatti namarupa paccaya nama) by 2 modes Namely, psychic supports (arammana paccaya) and decisive dependence (upanisssaya paccaya). That is, it is mental and physical objects which determine personality's consciousness and future, and the character of personality is decisively dependent on the physical - mental environment.

Sixthly, mentality-formations serve as the base for the arising of mentality-formations (namarupa paccaya namarupa) by 9 modes. Namely, predominance (adhipati paccaya), co-nascence (sahajata paccaya), reciprocity (annamanna paccaya), character-istic dependence (nissaya paccaya), nutriment (ahara paccaya), controlling faculty (indriya paccaya), disassociation factors (vippayutta paccaya), presence factors (atthi paccaya), appearance-continuance factors (avigata paccaya).

(1) continuity by momentum (anantara paccaya) implies that each occasion of contact is objectified in the next occasion which arises, and there is no break between, not even in sleep, but that one mental impulsion is followed by another without a pause, and it is this mode of conditionality which perpetuates mentality in life or in so - called death.

(2) continuity by immediacy (samanantara paccaya). This is of the same order as the preceding mode, only its function is more direct. Whereas the first mode is general in scope, the second applies to the particular. In the first instance one flash of mentality is followed by another flash merely as a matter of general function, in the second instance it is in direct sequence. That is, with each contact (phassa) sensation (vedana) immediately follows. Thus it is that these two modes of conditionality clarify how the present moment perishes and how the future moment becomes, by an objectification process.

(3) frequency of volitional impulsion (asevana paccaya). This too is of the same order as the above two. However, its function is not only automatic but is volitional. It signifies will (cetana), one volitional impulsion (javana) being followed by the next (up to seven in the normal consciousness, six impulsions in some cases, five at the death - moment), whereon a fresh cycle of seven impulsions begins. There are altogether 55 kinds of volitional mentality accompanied by the 52 concomitants of consciousness. 12 are unwholesome (akusala), being dominated by greed, hate, and delusion. 21 are wholesome (kusala): 8 being mundane, 5 pertaining to the brahma - consciousness, 4 to the arupa - brahma consciousness, and 4 to the supramundane. 18 are functional and pertain to the emancipated consciousness (kiriya). 4 are supra-mundane resultants (vipaka).

(4) association factors (sampayutta paccaya). This implies that mentality is always accompanied by its concomitants (cetasikas) by a fourfold process, covering all the 89 kinds of consciousness (citta). Namely, they arise together (eka - uppatta), perish together (eka - nirodha), possess the same support (eka - arammana), and partake of the same element (eka - vatthuka). Mentality is therefore the base for mentality by this mode of process.

(5) receptacle of voidness (natthi paccaya). What is implied is that all factors of mentality (or physicality) function in a locus of emptiness. Were it not for this voidness there would be no place for anything to arise. It is by the very absence of obstructing material that consciousness (or physicality) is possible of projection. Thus it is that the receptacle of voidness is a prime factor of conditionality by very nature of its basic necessity.

20

(6) continuity by disappearance (vigata paccaya). This mode is of the nature of direction, of a proceeding forth, and is thus similar to the first two modes. All mentality possesses direction, even the seeming aimlessness of most minds being itself a form of direction, of movement, of going. Thus is it a mode.

The above six modes (1 - 6) function in mentality as base for further mentality.

(7) root causality (hetu paccaya). The root causality is ethical in content and compulsive in aim. It determines greed (lobha), hate (dosa), and delusion (moha), together with their opposites of non - greed (alobha), non - hate (adosa), and non-delution (amoha). It is of prime import, because all mentality and formations have their roots in either wholesome or unwholesome material. The root causality determines the whole color, tone, and outlook of the trend of personality, mental and physical.

(8) concentrated absorption (jhana paccaya). This mode has influence over 79 kinds of consciousness, excluding 10 non - caused resultants (tvi - panca vinnana ahetuka vipaka cittani). Concentrated absorption is comprised of 5 concomitants of consciousness: reasoning (vittakha), reflection (vicara), bliss (piti), feeling (vedana), and one - pointedness of concentration (ekaggata), These are able to regulate the process of mentality and formations by a powerful determining force.

(9) path means (magga paccaya). This mode determines whether the stream of personality is merely mundane (lokiya) or tends to the supramundane (lokuttara). Its influence is on 71 kinds of consciousness, excuding 18 ethically uncaused kinds (ahetuka cittani). The path means is comprised of 8 concomitants of consciousness. wisdom (panna), reasoning (vittakha), right speech (samma vaca), right activity (samma kammanta), right means of livelihood (samma ajiva), energy (viriya), mindfulness (sati), and one-pointed concentration (ekaggata).

(10) immediate volitional causality (kamma paccaya). This mode has influence on all the 89 kinds of consciousness by one concomitant: will (cetana). It is, therefore, of the nature of a compulsive force and comprehensive in scope.

(11) resultancy (vipaka paccaya). This mode is ethical in tone and has influence over only 36 kinds of consciousness. 15 are ethically uncaused (ahetuka). 8 are wholesome though mundane (kamavacara mahavipaka), 5 are brahma-like (rupavacara vipaka), 4 are arupa-brahma like (arupavacara vipaka), and 4 are supramundane resultants (lokuttara vipaka). It is these resultant kinds of consciousness which take rebirth in a womb whensoever their time is ripe.

The above five modes (7-11) function in mentality as base for further mentality and form.

(12) consequence (paccajata paccaya). As already stated earlier, this mode which represents mentality, supports the body which arises after it, otherwise the body would not be able to continue as a living organism. Mentality arises first, followed by the organism, which is its consequence.

This one mode (12) serves in mentality as the base for form.

(13) antecedence (purejata paccaya). Again, the organism which is born into the world serves in turn as the base for the arising of fresh mentality. It is what the body and its senses gather for it that enables the mind to absorb fresh data and continue.

This one mode (13) serves in form as the base for mentality.

(14) psychic support (arammana paccaya). Mental and physical objects are absorbed by the mind as psychic supports and determine its future thereby. This mode of conditionality covers a wide field and influences all the 89 kinds of consciousness and the 52 concomitants thereof. Even Nibbana is included in this mode. The supports, of course, are absorbed through the sixfold data field. Thus, there are visible supports (ruparammana), sounds (saddarammana), odours (gandharammana), flavours (rasarammana), tangibles (photthabbarammana), and intangibles (dhammarammana). These are comprehensive in scope and influence all mentality.

(15) decisive characteristic dependence (upanissaya paccaya). This mode determines the character of the mentality, and like the above mode is comprehensive in scope. It is decisive because its function is immediate, and is also integrated as traits of character, which serves as future dependence for the mind.

22

The above 2 modes (14 - 15) serve for mentality - and - form as base for mentality.

(16) predominance (adhipati paccaya). This mode has influence over 84 kinds of consciousness, excluding 2 hate-dominated, 2 delusion-dominated, and 1 unwholesome physical suffering consciousness. Its concomitants are 37, excluding hate, envy, avarice, and doubt. There are 4 predominant qualities besides (zeal, energy, thought, and investigation) which influence 52 kinds of consciousness, comprising 8 of greed, 2 of hate, 8 of mundane benefit, 8 of mundane functionality, 10 pertaining to the brahma- gods, 8 to the arupa-brahma gods, and 8 supramundane.

(17) co-nascence (sahajata paccaya). This mode covers all the 89 kinds of consciousness and the 52 concomitants. In that mentality and its concomitants arise together they take heading under this mode of conditionality.

(18) reciprocity (annamanna paccaya). Not only does mentality and its concomitants arise together, they are reciprocal in function and activate each other accordingly as well as simultaneously.

(19) characteristic dependence (nissaya paccaya). This mode is of a resultant nature and applies to characteristic traits of mentality brought over from a previous life. Thus it determines the nature of the personality which prevails in the immediate life.

(20) nutriment (ahara paccaya). This implies both coarse food (rupahara) as well as mental sustenance (namahara). Mental sustenance is threefold, and is comprised of contact, will, and consciousness.

(21) controlling faculty (indriya paccaya). This mode may be divided into two groups, physical controlling faculties (rupindriya), and mental controlling faculties (namindriya). The physical pertain to the eye, ear, nose, tongue, body, female, and male faculties. The mental pertain to the mind, vitality, suffering, pleasure, grief, joy, equanimity, faith, energy, mindfulness, concentration, wisdom, aspiration to supramundane knowledge, knowledge, and release knowledge faculties. These, of course, play a great part in the determination of the direction in which personality is to develop.

(22) disassociation (vippayutta paccaya). This implies that even though mentality is of a different nature from physicality, they nevertheless influence each other by their very functions of disassociation. They do not arise together or perish together (mentality arises faster and perishes faster than physicality by 17 instants), nevertheless they interact on each other in between intervals (before and after) thereof.

(23) presence (atthi paccaya). This mode covers the other modes of co - nascence, antecedence, consequence, nutriment, and controlling faculty. These are all presence factors in the sense of immediate existence. Thus, this mode of conditionality is a general one and comprehensive in scope.

(24) non - disappearance continuance (avigata paccaya). This is of the same nature as the above, in that if mind and form continue then they are present as a condition, and although they may arise and perish from moment to moment nevertheless preserve a semblance of motionlessness. Mentality and formations thus serve as the base for mentality and formations under this mode of conditionality.

The above nine modes (16 - 24) serve for mentality - and - form as base for further mentality - and - form.

Of all these modes of conditionality, four are all - inclusive, taking in all phenomena (paramattha dhamma) which endures. The four are objective psychic support (arammana paccaya), decisive characteristic dependence (upanissaya paccaya), immediate volitional causality (kamma paccaya), and presence mode (atthi paccaya).

Thus it is that mentality and formations depend for their arising and perpetuity on these modes of conditionality. They also serve as the base for the consequent split of personality.

To put an end to this kind (anatta) of disintegration of personality, the stream - enterer (sotapanna) or once- returner (sa- kadagamin), has to submerge his peripheral faculties at diaphragm- pit and press on until the integration of emancipation (arahatta- ship) is attained. Until this is achieved, he is still a *sekhapuggala*, one who has still some training to undergo. And here again we have Buddha's advice :

"There are three factors, O Bhikkhus, necessary for one intent on the attainment of the higher consciousness (adhicitta). Namely, the factors of concentration, of energy, and of equanimity."

By the potential of these three factors, the elemental (dhatu) portion of the human aggregate is processed and transmuted, until it emerges in pure form. The essence (dhamma) portion is processed, until it emerges in perfect qualities of consciousness (parami). The elemental portion is the end - result of the transmuted cognitive (vinnana) base. The essence portion is the fusion of aeonic experience into a specific field of personality as signified by the Dhammakaya. Element and essence fuse in a specific field, to issue in the establishment of a state of being which from mundane has become supramundane.

IN REPLY TO LETTERS RECEIVED

Regarding your first question about 'psychic offshoots', it is not *explicitly* stated in the Pali Canon, but it is definitely *implicit* therein. To understand why it is not explicitly stated, one has only to notice the noble silence which Buddha preserved when Vaccha-gotta the wandering ascetic questioned him on whether the self is eternal or not. How can something which arises by way of circumstantial occasion be eternal or non-existent? In fact, the Buddha had no time to spare in expounding such an intricate subject, of prolonged metaphysical disquisition, of talking over the heads of his audience, when the audience was already obviously beyond its depth. For the doctrine is profound, even in its appearance profound, to be understood only by the wise: it is hard for you, coming from a different background, a different set of teachers, tendencies, etc. This is the standard reply of the Master, waiving away something which he knew to be beyond the grasp of the average worldling. As a matter of fact, because of its depth the Abhidhamma was propounded in the deva world and not the human world.

The doctrine of split-personality, as I would call it, is implicit in the formula of dependent origination (paticca samuppada) as found in the Abhidhamma. Freshly enlightened, we witness the Buddha contemplating it, in direct order and inverse. It is primarily through contact (phassa) that new forms of consciousness arise. They arise because it is in the very nature of five-fold consciousness (panca vinnana ahetuka vipaka citta) to arise when there is already an antecedent level in existence. The original rebirth-consciousness (patisandhi vinnana) serves as the base for its arising, and its arising is either wholesome or unwholesome (kusala-akusala) because each flicker of consciousness which arises is imbued with the environ-mental ethical flavour from which it takes its rise. Thus, streams of consciousness vary and fluctuate from moment to moment in the record of their ethical content. The offshoots of personality are to be found in the 18 ahetuka vipaka cittani section of the 89 categories of consciousness, although all vipaka levels have their own part to play.

The immediate resultants of psychic activity as they arise through the five-fold consciousness, resolve themselves into the contact receptacle (sampaticchana) and on into the observing receptacle (santirana), which can be either kusala or akusala. Although these two streams (kusala-akusala) of the panca-vinnana sampaticchana, and santirana citta are merely functional and are causeless (ahetuka), that is automatic, they are streams which possess a fivefold-charge. Namely, to depart (cuti), to relink (patisandhi), to become subconscious (bhavanga), to observe (santirana), and to persevere as memory (tadarammana). It is here, therefore, that the offshoot doctrine is to be dug. Namely, in the pancadvaravajjana, the pancavinnana, the sampaticchana, and the santirana uppekha.

I cannot help regretting sometimes that although there in no lack of study of the Abhidhamma, deep penetration into it aided by jhanic insight is not practiced, and therefore the general understanding of it is too superficial to be of value, and too often degenerates into mere wordy gymnastics. This is why ariyas differ from the worldling. It is the first test of his concentrated insight that a sotapanna observes the currents of his consciousness peripherally rising and vanishing from second to second, thus abandoning belief in permanent selfhood (sakkayaditthi). Although he is still unable to dispel passion, he realizes that he has to do something better before he can ever bless himself with a self worthy of the name. It is obvious that the offshoot doctrine in no way shakes the doctrine of kamma, but complements it. It is the cumulative nucleus of the antecedent relinking consciousness (patisandhi citta) which receives the weight of past and present kamma, offshoots receive only the surplus, are left only with the dregs, the main stream having taken off with the draught.

In reply to question 2. There cannot be said to be anything 'absolute' about the origin of these split - personalities or offshoot-streams of consciousness, because an antecedent main-stream itself began as a substream. It is termed a main - stream only in the sense of its antecedence, to distinguish it from its offshoots which sprout therefrom, offshoots which antecedent to this never so much as existed. That is why we have Buddha refusing to affirm one way or the other, whether the self is eternal or not. The offshoot never existed before, how can it be eternal? It cannot

27

be said to be destroyed either, because from henceforth it continues on a life of its own   In short, *which* self are you talking about?   It is obvious that this doctrine, in Buddha's time as well as our own, will hardly be appreciated by the many, for no one likes to think of himself as splitting at death here and there in space.

However, the process goes back endlessly, and no 'absolute' appears, for a person who practices jhanic recollection of past births, is able to recollect only so far as the moment he became an offshoot.   He can't recall beyond that, because antecedent to that he never so much as existed.   Of course, a stream which has preserved its potential for aeons is obviously more developed and of a higher order than its immediate offshoots, which have only the immediate life removed to refer to.   Some can trace their psychic ancestry countless aeons back, as for the general run of people living in the world today they are mostly just beginning on the road to psychic evolution: that is, recent offshoots of this present age.   It is obvious that to talk to them about metaphysical matters will leave or excite no response, because they possess no antecedent store of knowledge on which to fall back on. All previous knowledge accumulates in the bhavanga receptacle.   Men talk of genius, but the name is only for something which they do not comprehend, as though he were a freak.   But all things arise through bases, through contacts, through causes, and through conditions, and do not arise from nothing.   A man is a genius simply because be built up in a certain line through a series of lives, and his ability is merely a manifestation of what went before.

In another sense, it all depends on the initial start.   That is, how the offshoot takes its rise, and from what material it springs. The offshoot of a Plato will surely have kinship with intelligence, and the offshoot of a dunce kinship with duncehood.   This will be their kammic heritage, since all aggregates of personality start off with kamma, being kamma-vipaka consciousness, developing thereby for good or ill.   This explains the difference in basic dispositions and levels of intelligence, some commencing on a high scale and others the reverse.

Regarding the third matter.   I should say that your interpretation of the anatta doctrine as found in your book has similar accents insofar as integration is concerned.   However, it is difficult

to conclude with you that anatta and atta are the same.   Buddhas
and Arahattas inhabit pure space above the highest arupa - brahma
loka, in ascending scale.   Each previous Buddha is one section
higher than his successor down the line of Buddhahood.   They
inhabit Nibbana as complete beings, as super-selves   They are not
submerged in any ocean of selflessness or forgetfulness. One Buddha
is quite distinct from another, even as the Arahattas who gather
round their Master   They have 'attas' because they are no more
reborn. Because rebirth in the world begets offshoots, this is anatta.
A stream of consciousness cannot be blessed with the name of atta
when it can hardly control its immediate destiny, but is flung here
and there in space without any knowledge of what went before or
what is to come.

     (1) *The relation of the parami-self to the bhavanga.* All cons-
cious selves (the parami-self inclusive) must be complemented by an
unconscious stream (even as light and dark complement each other),
because when consciousness flickers into existence it almost immediately (except in jhana) flickers back into subconsciousness   This is
its cycle and natural mode   If there were no bhavanga the mind
would never be able to rest at all.   The collective experience of the
parami-self cannot be to the fore of consciousness in its completeness
at any given moment. What is not to the fore is sunk and collected
in a receptacle which is the bhavanga, its subconscious otherness.
Perhaps I failed to make myself explicit, but when it is said that the
peripheral mind must be sunk down into the bhavanga, what is
actually meant is to sink it down and then edge it up two finger -
breadths *above* the bhavanga (see Samma Ditthi pg. 47 - 49).   If it
is not edged up thus there will be no full awareness, there will only
be submergence into the ceaseless random flow of the subconscious
stream.   It is edged up thus so as to be near the bhavanga stream,
so that it can dip into it at will, just as one dips into a stream and
retrieves flowing objects therein.   It is correct to say that by so
doing the peripheral mind is deepened and made aware of experiences
unplumbed before (brought over from other lives, as well as
opening new horizons which may arise).   It is also correct to say
that it is the redemption of the subconscious by making it conscious
No, it is not assumed that the sleeping consciousness is the truest
and purest.   It is indeed the seat of the irrational.   But this is only

29

because the stream itself is uncontrolled and impure. If it were controlled and pure (as in the nirodha samapatti of the arahatta) then it would indeed be the highest. When it is advised to sink the peripheral faculties down (and edged up) there consciously, it is firstly to recover lost experience embedded therein, to integrate all that experience, to smelt away and purge the dross, and to intensify it into pure awareness. This implies that the bhavanga of the ordinary man and the emancipated one differ: one being unrestrained and impure, the other lucid and refined. Because his subconscious is pure the arahatta has no delusive or morbid dreams. This is the relation of the parami-self to the bhavanga.

(2) It is known perfectly well to those who practice the Dhammakaya concentration that the centre two finger-breadths above the navel is of crucial significance. It is just because the peripheral mind is unable to integrate itself at this point that it splits off at death. It is just because the arahatta achieves his stand here that he takes off without a split. The Buddha taught in-and-out breathing meditation so as to lure consciousness to this point, for it is observed that when one takes a deep breath it is to this region that the mind is lured. The only drawback is that people confuse the issue and concentrate on the peripheral nose. Besides, breathing is also a means of purifying the mental as well as the physical factors of the organism.

(3) There is no permanent maximum of three offshoots. Each offshoot (on rebirth and consequent death) becomes in turn a so-called main-stream with future offshoots. And so on ad infinitum. It is clearer to say that each life is a combination of four streams. That there are 20 characteristic frequencies (akara) of 4 stream or heaps (sankhepa) of personality is to be analyzed in the light of the formula of dependent origination (paticca samuppada).

Firstly, there is the aggregate stream of the past life (akusala-kusala vipaka) which descends to rebirth in a womb. This is a fivefold aggregate stream comprising of ignorance (avijja), psychic data (sankharas), desire (tanha), grasping tendencies (upadana), and mental impulsions of becoming (bhava).

Secondly, we have the aggregate stream which, once the first stream has fused in the womb, gives rise to another fivefold set which is purely resultant in status (ahetuka vipaka). This is

30

comprised of consciousness (vinnana), mentality and physicality (nama-rupa), the six sense-group (salayatana), contact facility (phassa), and feeling (vedana). Their status is purely receptive and negative, and at birth are devoid of immediate ethical responsibility.

Thirdly, as environmental contact is established, another fivefold set accumulates, whose function is immediate and positive (akusala-kusala). It is comprised of desire (tanha), grasping (upadana), becoming (bhava), ignorance (avijja), and psychic data (sankharas) It is this third stream which accumulates fresh kamma, and condenses it down into the two preceding streams, leaving an impress therein. Although the two preceding streams are negative in nature insofar as this present existence is concerned their influence on the third party is basic, as in the status of parent to offspring, for were it not for them there would be no arising of a third party at all.

Fourthly, the third stream serves as the base for the arising of another fivefold set which is futuristic in content (akusala-kusala vipaka). That is, a negative group for future rebirth and reception of impressions. That is, consciousness (vinnana), mentality-and-physicality (nama-rupa), the six sense-group (salayatana), contact (phassa), and feeling (vedana).

At death, due to lack of integration and purification at one firmly poised and oriented centre, these four heaps of personality make a total split and go their ways.

(4) The nature of the transcendence of the new self that arises. It is not to be considered as inherent in individuality, for that would be tantamount to championing the doctrine of a permanent soul flowing on unchanged, from some primordial source. It is indeed created by self-action but by no means is the self which created it originally transcendent. It is not a matter of *original* transcendence but *transmutation* (one would not call a piece of dirty carbon a brilliant diamond, and yet a brilliant diamond is composed of carbon). There is no infinite regress into some aboriginal uncreated transcendent element insofar as selfhood is concerned, because self-hood does not arise in this wise. It arises through contact and desire.

(5) Will is not worn out finally by knowledge. It is certain that will is transformed by knowledge and knowledge deepened by right will. It is probably as you say that the writer is speaking of the will (thirst) to exist in this world of amorphous plurality.

(6) Regarding the role of percepts. Percepts are indeed incipient selves (sankharas) but they are restricted to four groups (as referred to in answer No 3). Altogether there can be only four in one life-time, because of the fivefold aggregate restriction (namely, a form, perception, memory, thought-process, knowing faculty). All these four groups must possess form, perception, memory, thought-process, and knowing faculty to be able to form a centre of recognized oriented selfhood. Mere flickerings of consciousness alone are insufficient to be recognized as self, they have to be grouped in the fivefold combination as stated. They are now in function as sub-centers of consciousness, in the waking state, the sleeping state, and in the dream state.

The sleeping self may be regarded as the *first* party, the collective subconscious. The dreaming self is the *second* party. The waking self is the *third* party. The dying self is the *fourth* party. These are all projections of each other. That is, their interaction is reciprocal, because they are held together in one organic field. At death, however, there is no check to their separative tendencies, the organism having given way. Because of this instability of all personalities, we have Buddha in the Mahasatipatthana Sutta advising us to observe (in jhana) form in form, feeling in feeling, consciousness in consciousness, and mental essences in mental essences, and to then integrate them all. Without this fivefold combination they would be merely states of consciousness with no field of orientation. However, the waking self and the dreaming self are distinct. Frames of internal-external reference do (in the normal man) split the experience and the desire. This is just the same as saying that the personality is split essentially, because in the normal man the personality is always split by desire and a grasping after new satisfactions as well as a hankering after old. Because of grasping, becoming. It is only the integrated man (arahatta) who is so able to gather all his past experience from the corners of his bhavanga stream and dip into any region of it at will, not by any random contact or external compulsion.

32

As for the parami-consciousness observing its own arising, it may be termed a super-percept observing another percept. It does not actually, however, witness its own arising. It arises first reflexively without being witnessed, and sinks back into bhavanga. It is retrieved from bhavanga by a subsequent consciousness through its own momentum. It is the subsequent consciousness which does the observing then. It is only after a certain state of consciousness has arisen that the subsequent consciousness observes what has passed. This is called reviewing (paccavekkhana) consciousness. Therefore, it is correct to say that it is one percept observing another percept, a succeeding one reviewing a preceding one. There is no question of a static permanent super-consciousness observing. It is a later series of states (taking place in the fivefold combination of form, feeling, perception, memory, and knowledge faculty) observing an already arisen (and then bhavanga) series of states. Personality can review itself (and know) only one step or more at a remove. It can never know itself the *immediate* moment it arises. This is why the word *present* has always to be qualified by three modes: present by moment, present by continuity, present by delimited extent. Because a human being is a composite of all these modes he is misled to think that his self is one and identical at all times, immortal in fact. Indeed, percepts imbued with the vital principle (jivitindriya) are hard to understand. If they were easy Buddha would surely not have corrected Ananda when that disciple expressed the opinion that the formula of dependent origination was clear and easy to understand. On the contrary, Buddha replied, it was profound, even in its appearance profound. Buddha himself, fresh in enlightenment, devoted a whole week of concentration to it alone.

(7) All conscious or unconscious states are temporary (nirodha samapatti inclusively). True, the arahatta returns to normal personal life. But a distinction must be drawn. His faculties are lucent and pure, unlike the normal man. Although the arahatta sees things, touches and tastes them, he does not hanker after them, having rendered hankering extinct, viewing things with equanimity. This kind of equanimity is called calanga upekkha.

The arahatta does not backslide from Nirvanic attainment because he has already rendered the root defilements extinct.

Besides, he has been trained to be on the alert, until his mind has become so by nature, and he dies (leaves the body) in full awareness of mind. This is the true arahatta.

However, those who practice the Dhammakaya meditation may attain to the arahatta form and consciousness, but they are not classed as arahattas. They are not because they fail to render the defilements extinct. They simply have a foretaste in meditation of what the arahatta consciousness is like, and later return to normal consciousness. The temporary validity of the arahatta form and consciousness (mentioned in Samma Samadhi I) applies to this type of practitioner, not the real arahatta. As for this aspirant, he has not only a fourfold personality - plurality as in the normal man, but altogether 18 forms and levels (as given in S.S. I). Before he dies he concentrates all these forms and levels (sheath in sheath) into one (at navel centre) and takes off to the brahma world or deva world. Consequently, there is no split as in the normal man. So it is to be understood that not only the arahatta but also jhanic laymen are able to die without a personality - split taking place. This is because these laymen have trained themselves in the Dhammakaya concentration and die in full awareness. The great significance of this system of meditation, therefore, unlike other meditations, is obvious. As for the normal layman who knows nothing of meditation, his levels of consciousness are on the desire plane, and his destiny likewise.

(8) By immediate physical rebirth being rare is implied that an interval of at least a few days takes place. There is no such thing as an immediate jumping from the death-bed into the womb (except in jhanic adepts). There is never *any* impulsion to physical rebirth as such. The impulsion arises from the native's own grasping desire to be so born (to taste physical pleasures anew), and he cannot remain permanently disembodied because he doesn't possess the heart to remain so. In the case of the higher devas, they cannot remain so because either their merit (gas-like) or life-span has been exhausted and leaves them flat. They have no choice but to be reborn.

(9) Buddhas in their ayatanas are constantly available to help beings, human or otherwise. They can be termed god-equivalents if the terminology suits. It is mostly a matter of

34

terminology which divides the human race in the matter of religion. Most people believe in higher beings, it is only the concepts and the attributes which differ in kind. Regarding Buddhas in their ayatanas much could be said which would make not only people of other faiths but so - called Buddhists open their eyes.

On page 3 of your paper you mention that the four heap theory differs from the fivefold personality group. This is not so at all. Each so-called heap is a fivefold group in itself. There are therefore 4 fivefold groups, not one. In your Postscript you say that a psychic offshoot is not one of the elements of the fivefold 'pseudo-self'. As a matter of fact, each offshoot has form, feeling, perception, mental aggregates, and consciousness. It is always so wrong in Buddhist circles to reduce everything to a naked kamma thrust. It is not that naked at all. Offshoots, like their parent, are full-bodied personalities, even if psychic ones. They are indeed selves, if ever-changing ones. It is because personality can be reproduced and divided so easily, that is why the Buddha emphasized the impersonality of becoming, not because of its 'nakedness'.

Regarding the multiplicity of selves, those with jhanic attain - ment can through mind-control even multiply their mind-bodies much further. In the Pali it can easily be found that the adept if he so wants 'being one becomes many, being many he becomes one'. Buddha informs Potthapada how one can 'get three kinds of self: a physical self, a mind - form self, and a formless self' The physical self is easily understood. As for the mind-form self, it is stated that it 'has a form and is made of mind, complete in all its limbs, possessed of supersense organs'. The formless self is the arupa - brahma consciousness. Because most Buddhists hardly practice concentration so as to know things for themselves, they will never grasp the doctrine of anatta, not to mention Nibbana. They may grasp something of impermanence and suffering but not the latter.

As for N's failing to understand the connection of psychic offshoots with the formula of dependent origination, it is a prime drawback of all Buddhists, not only Theravadins. For it is here that the profundity of the doctrine lies and to which Buddha refers when he admonishes Ananda that the doctrine cannot be clear to

35

the normal man. Buddhists, especially scholars, don't seem to realize that Buddha rates contact (phassa) as of fundamental importance. In Samma Ditthi page 64, I quoted Buddha stating that regarding dhamma the root of it is will, that it arises whenever attention is focussed on it, and that it appears through sense - contact. Indeed we have to expand the term 'contact' beyond its traditional explanation if we are to do the anatta doctrine justice. It is contact which divides personality. A man one moment through contact in a certain environment receives a certain set of impressions, the next moment receives in some other environment another totally different set. He may through this random contact become strongly attached (upadana) to both and hanker (tanha) after them in his mind because they both afford him pleasure (sukha vedana). This is the root of split- personality in its rudimentary form, and if unchecked by restraining reflection may deteriorate and even in this very life lead to unfortunate consequences. It is this amorphousness of the splitting process which engaged Buddha's attention at his enlightenment as well as the way of putting an end to the split.

This putting an end to the multiplication of the species may seem to the Western mind as unnatural and nihilistic, but for the enlightened Buddhist the multiplication of ignorance and suffering and evil can hardly be something to be desired. The contrast is too great: the blundering entry into existence so quick and easy, and the way to release so slow and hard. Why bring unnecessary suffering into the world if it can be avoided?

On page 6 you mention Buddha's inaccessible Nirvana. Buddha's Nirvana is not inaccessible as it may seem, for access can be gained thereto if the proper technique is applied. On page 8 you say that 'true self - integration' is a phrase distinctly not Theravadin. Rather, we have Buddha repeating over and over again phrases of similar import: 'Which is better, to go in search of a woman or to go in search of your self?' 'Be unto your self an isle and refuge'. 'Self is the refuge of self'. It is to the integrated self of the emancipated one that the Buddha is always pointing. 'He who has his mind firmly established no Mara can shake'.

As for the phrase 'devoid of immediate ethical responsibility' what is implied is that since this offshoot is a new one it can know nothing of the past, and we cannot hold a baby in its cradle responsible for any unethical action, since it can know nothing at this stage of ethics.

As for the remark regarding the Buddhist community deciding upon the orthodoxy or heresy of 'my theories', it is something which may be amusing, because the Buddhist community is so split and unstable that it can never express any judgement worth considering. The so - called experts are unable to fling away their preconceived notions and actually get down to practice. The doctrines which I have referred to may seem new to scholars, but as truths understood by Buddhas and noble disciples they are as old as the universe is old. I have proposed nothing new at all, but rather these doctrines have been imposed on me as the result of prolonged investigation. It is not book - learning which clarifies doctrines, but the understanding which one brings thereto, revealing old doctrines in fresh light.

You mention that the split - personality theory does not accord with the traditional karmic doctrine. What is never grasped in Buddhist circles is that karma does not pertain to a single personality. As there are streams of personality so also are there streams of karma. The bulk of karma is condensed into the first heap, the other three heaps preserve only the residue. For it is the first heap that is to be built into the parami - self. The other selves have only the immediate life to refer to, they have no extensive 'background' except the present one. Their destiny is therefore necessarily limited. That is why these offshoots cling to the place of birth or the graveyard. They know no other higher sphere of orientation or reference. Of course, for them their self is the only real one they know. Their karma as a consequence is also only of the shallow type. In fact, these offshoots and their karma are of the inferior sort and not worth much consideration.

Integration in no way signifies 'utter cessation of selfhood'. If it were so, it would be a contradiction in terms, for one does not integrate oneself through a process of aeons merely to disintegrate again into some ocean of forgetfulness. Super - selfhood is just the end - result of the aeonic process, and Buddhas at the moment in Nibbana are certainly imbued with consciousness or they wouldn't be what they are. Their radiance fills the ocean of Nibbana... The attainment of Nibbana, of course, can be reached only through samadhi, and for that practice is essential.

To those who practice meditation and are in contact with other planes, it becomes increasingly difficult to communicate anything of deep significance. There is certainly more to Buddhism than meets the eye. The Buddha compared the leaves in his hand to those in the forest. The forest will always contain more than the leaves in one small hand. Sometimes it becomes dangerous to enter the forest...

Regarding Question 1: I cannot have been influenced by Madame Blavatsky because, although I have heard of her, I have never come across any of her books. Dr. C. being a scholar, it is only natural that he should conclude any knowledge gained as having its source in books. Scholars do not seem to realize that there are other sources of knowledge, and that it becomes tiresome to haggle over truths which, although they cannot be seen by the majority, nevertheless are so old and commonplace as to be taken for granted by the informed few.

Question 2 & 3: I will not say that the disembodied split-off self cannot be re-split, because I do know of cases when they can. But these cases are so rare that they can be dismissed from happening in general. As far as I know, they only occur at rare intervals in those great devas who are bodhisattas building paarmis, who through a supreme wish, at the moment of their descent from the deva plane to earth (to build more parami) split off and enter two wombs. After death of the two main-streams, they are again rejoined in the deva world. This is very rare, and does not occur in the ordinary disembodied spirit at all.

Mr. B. discusses the question of whether the mind is a function of the brain at length. It is unfortunate that through lack of data Mr. S. is unable to explain himself. It is known to only a very few Buddhists that the brain centre and the rebirth mind centre (haddaya vatthu) are located at two different levels in the

38

physical organism. From looking at the diagram it will be noticed that the rebirth mind - centre is referred to the diaphragm - pit two finger - breadths above the navel. Due to this two - level split in the mental locus, there is never any total integration of personality, and the reason why people often behave like two different persons altogether, in proportion to the predominance of one over the other at various times. At death there is a complete split between personalities, each possessing different kammas henceforth. If Bourne had died while he was A. J. Brown both of their person-alities would have survived. This is one reason why populations increase, a factor which Mr. B. asks Buddhists to explain. He is right to demand that Buddhists should grapple with these problems.

Mr. B. wishes to know why if consciousness can exist by itself that the brain is necessary as an instrument? It is not *necessary* as such, but merely the fact that through the force of kamma and *desire* consciousness seeks re - entry into a womb. Thus the consequent physicality which issues. People are born at all through the very propulsive force of *not being able to resist* a renewed physical existence. Adepts in jhana do not depend on the brain receptacle at all so long as they are absorbed in jhana, at death dispensing with it altogether.

Because the mental aggregates have two seats of focus, the peripheral brain centre is unable to remember anything in the matter of past existences. It cannot do so because it has no past births at all, before the present birth it never so much as existed. Mr. B. is right to say that at birth the brain is empty, it gathers impressions only later from environmental contact. The diaphragm centre (the so - called unconscious) preserves the record of past existences. To recall these the peripheral mind has to sink down to diaphragm level, or the latter has to arise to the peripheral level, before contact can be established. This is sometimes achieved through accidental contact, when some external sense data serves as the spark. Plato deals with this matter in his Phaedo. It is because ordinary human beings are unable to integrate their per-sonalities by an involuted technique that a total split occurs at death.

As for the rejection of soul, Buddha did not classify anything bodied or disembodied as such because to do so would be to exalt it to the status of changelessness and identicality, when in fact all physical and mental properties, bodied or disembodied, are in process of arising and perishing from second to second.

There is much concerning the supernormal which cannot be said here, which would make not Mr. B. but Buddhists themselves open their eyes. Very few Buddhists understand their religion because they cannot concentrate deep enough. If they were to do so, which is hardly likely, they will discover depths unplumbed before, and their whole concept of what Buddhism really is will be altered a great deal.

But at least these Buddhists are better off than Mr. B., they have faith, which is a quality not to be supercilious of, the first of a set of five (faith, ardour, mindfulness, concentration, and wisdom) essential for a true perspective of life.

***

The extent to which a teacher is necessary... Indeed, people do have an incredible capacity for seeing all sorts of lights, colours, shapes, sizes, etc. That is where the qualified teacher comes in. If he is qualified at all, he will be able to perceive in meditation whether the novice is on the right track or not. We cannot dismiss all the things which people see in meditation as mere hallucination. Of course, many of them are. But generalizations on the subject are deceptive , to say the least. Each case has to be taken in hand by the teacher qualified to do so...

The matter of the Nimitta. We omitted mention of the preliminary moving of the nimitta through the centres to simplify matters and to avoid confusion. We have known some, after they have already sunk the peripheral faculties down to the seventh position, to be jolted out thereof, and to start all over again from the nostril. This is a tedious and superfluous process. All that is necessary is to plunge the peripheral faculties down to centre and fix it there. Of course, most people find it extremely difficult at the first start to fix consciousness at the sixth or the seventh position, because it is so deep. That is why in-and-out-breathing (anapanasati) is generally recommended in the Scriptures, because it is easier to concentrate on the breath. Nevertheless, when breathing becomes refined, fades away, and finally stops, it is to the sixth position

40

(void centre) that the peripheral faculties sink, rising thence to the seventh position, and there stopped. Whence the sphere of Pathama Magga is perceived ...

The sphere of Pathama Magga (First Step) in its beginnings may appear as a mere star-like nucleus, but when intimately approached presents itself as huge, a whole aura of light The normal size is approximately 3cm. in diameter. However, according to the capacity of the practitioner, it can be expanded to a diameter of 4 metres, The sphere, of course, pertains to the human form. However, the spheres which pertain to the celestial form, and all the other forms which follow, are even greater in expansion and size. Now the sphere of the Dhammakaya Arahatta, for instance, is 40 metres in diameter at its normal size. However, it can be expanded to an even more incredible breadth, so as to capacitate the world in its void centre.

Regarding the whole matter of the luminous sphere. It has to be spherical, bright, still, and present itself as clear. It often presents itself even clearer than daylight. As for the size, it does not matter. It may so happen that the aspirant perceives a huge sphere instead of a small one. The sphere perceived may not be that of the Pathama Magga, but one pertaining to a more devious form. If so, it does not matter. Just concentrate in the centre thereof, and carry on.

In most cases, however, it is only the small star-like nucleus which is perceived, and progress always seems held up there, to the despair of the aspirant. It implies that perception hasn't arrived at culmination point, is still immature, unripe. Or that the subject cannot approach close enough to perceive the sphere in its true proportions. However, with time and patience, the nucleus will one day present itself as a sphere.. It will have to be perceived as a sphere if anything further is to be done. And all the aspirant can do is not to despair and leave off ...

It is due to the very separative tendency of the peripheral faculties, always holding at a distance instead of sinking in to void centre (the sixth position), that the sphere presents itself as a blur, a star, or a mere jumping nucleus, or even not at all... It is best not to imagine or visualize anything. One has just to sink all the

41

peripheral faculties down to void centre and thence up to the seventh position)... This sphere of Pathama Magga, and all the other spheres which follow, are not only to be observed objectively as from a detached status, but to be merged into. It is only then that their true essences may be experienced.

The various spheres of Dhammanupassana satipatthana, Sila, Samadhi, etc., already contain the elements of mindfulness, morality, and so forth, respectively. All experience accumulated in past lives is contained in spheres, the sphere being the most self contained of forms. Of course, if these qualities of mindfulness, etc., are already there, they have still to be cultivated, developed, enlarged, and purified as one treads the path (Magga). The above spheres are the Noble Eightfold Path itself, and it is only through them that release is ever achieved. However, they can scarcely be said to be inherent or not to be inherent. They are certainly to be cultivated and enlarged.

One pronounces Samma Araham: Sa - ma Ar - ra - hung. And it means the perfect, or worthy one. Since the aim of meditation is perfection, the mind has to occupy itself with this ideal, keeping it to the fore, so that these qualities of perfection may arise as concentration becomes intense. Besides this, this word formula is a sort of mental signal to those higher spiritual beings in Nibbana by whom supernormal aid may be transmitted down.

You enquire regarding the nucleus of light expanding into a sphere. This sphere is in every creature, and you do not have to imagine it, because it is already where you are looking for it, in the seventh position as seen in the diagram. All creatures have this sphere in them or they would not be alive, for it is through this sphere that they were born at all. People do not perceive this sphere because from the time of birth onwards, all their activities are centred outside the body, not inside. When we attempt to concentrate, therefore, and sink our peripheral faculties down into the centre of the body, we cannot expect our attempts to be crowned with immediate success, because the mind has been so

42

accustomed by habit to perceive only things which are *outside*.
What is more, through contact with the external world, consciousness has become restless, crudified, and defiled, whence the keeness
of its perception has therefore been obscured thereby.

It is essential, therefore, to first calm and purify the faculties,
by sinking all attention to the centre inside. This, of course, is
extremely difficult at first, and all that may result is often a
sensation of whirling or groping in the dark. We have to be brave
and patient, and continue. We cannot expect to perceive light
immediately, even as a man going out from a brightly lighted
room into the dark outside cannot make out anything distinctly
at first.

You enquire, if the sphere appears blurred or flickers and
flits, how the default is to be corrected. There is only one way.
That is, to calm the body and mind by attempting to fix attention
on one point, upon the centre of the sphere, and keep it there
absolutely still. It will then slowly clarify by itself. Of course,
this is extremely difficult, because the sphere often manifests and
presents itself as a mere nucleus, upon which it is hard to concentrate. It appears small because of immaturity in meditation, for
if the peripheral mind were to approach closer thereto, this nucleus
will be revealed in its normal proportions as a sphere of 2 - 3 cm.
in diameter, large enough on which to concentrate...

Regarding the matter of the 'Bright Mark'. It is a vague
term, which conveys little sense. These so - called 'Bright Marks'
as you may notice from the booklet, are really spheres which
contain essential properties peculiar only to themselves. That is
to say, mindfulness (satipatthana), morality (sila), concentration
(samadhi), wisdom (panna), release (vimutti), and the perceptive-
knowledge of release (vimutti nana dassana). It is important to
know at which particular sphere (and to the especial form it
pertains) one is concentrating on at any particular moment, and
not class them all under some amorphous heading of 'Bright
Mark'. And this also applies for the term 'Body', which is mislea-
ding and inadequate, for each successive astral form possesses its
especial significance and name, not to be confused with the next.

43

Regarding the 'pin-point' or 'tiny diamond' which you say comes and goes. Yes, it is quite possible, and very necessary, to enlarge it... I have known some to take years before their efforts are crowned with visible success. On the other hand, others take only a few days .. We cannot hope for quick success, because the mind is by its very nature a precipitate thing, by habit rushing on in its random and fickle course. It need hardly be stressed, however, that our efforts are not being applied in vain...

These spheres are not a repetition, because each successive form (or level of consciousness) is imbued with a succession of spheres, in various increasing degrees of refinement. They are indeed different stages of attainment. The forms mentioned are not the result of auto-suggestion but are the result of the process as consciousness is pushed to its most translucent limit. As for the term Arupa - Brahma, it is understood that it does not imply lack of form but that the 'form-lessness' lies only in the attainments practiced. Namely, akasananca ayatana jhana, etc.

Unfortunately, we were not in a position to clarify all this in detail in the booklet, because these concentration exercises are something to be experienced rather than described. It is in view of this literal disadvantage (the ineffability of concentration attainments) that descriptions fail.

You express doubts regarding the concentration exercises, in view of their repetitiousness. Perhaps it would be as well to clarify that they are not variations on a simple theme constantly elaborated. The whole method is a process of pushing consciousness from its crudest mundane level to its translucent supramundane limits. This, of course, is something to be directly experienced to be appreciated. Each successive form and its respective spheres are different stages of attainment, in ever increasing degrees of refine-ment.

It will be appreciated, therefore, that the booklet was not intended for general reading but as a meditational manual. It is only after all the stages have been attained, and consciousness is

44

purified to its most translucent limit, that the attention is adverted to other attainments, such as the investigation and observation (in jhana) of the Four Noble Truths, etc...

You say that you have been able to perceive a misty sphere. That is good, fix attention on it and keep it there, until it clarifies and becomes bright, and translucent. On no account let it disappear, until another nucleus is seen in its centre, which again will manifest as a sphere as concentration becomes keen. You say a *black* mark appears. We have to expect such things. This black nucleus which you see is the evil in life, and whenever we meditate it does its best to overcome our minds in the darkness of ignorance, of greed, delusion, and hate. We have to be constantly on our guard against these evil forces (akusala dhamma) and extinguish them as soon as they manifest. This is why we witness Buddha's emphasis on mindfulness (satippatthana).

You say you see many *nimittas*. We have to take whatever nimitta that appears one at a time or else concentration wanders and strays, and the thread of the process is lost. We have to be prepared for all these manifestations, and not to be lured from our main objective... We should not allow any visions or landscapes to distract us from the main objective of arriving at the various forms and spheres, until finally the Dhammakaya form is perceived...

You express doubts about the method advocated... Of course we do not say release cannot be attained without jhana. There are two methods of release: panna - vimutti, and ceto - vimutti. Panna - vimutti is that method which obtains release through repeated (life after life) discrimination (vitakka - vicara) on the factors of impermanence, suffering, and impersonality, until attachment and the defilements (asavas) are winnowed away and finally exhausted. Attainment of release through this 'dry-bare' method (without jhana) is also called sukkha - vipassaka. Perhaps this is the method most congenial to the psychology of the West, due to its peripheral facility. Buddha himself, however, did not attain perfect enlightenment through this method (as some would like to suppose he did). And why? Because this is not the method of the All-Enlightened Buddhas. This method of sukkha-vipassaka does not endow the aspirant with all-enlightened knowledge or supernormal power, essential to a Buddha, who has to teach and convince. This method, however, is sufficient to winnow away the asavas, insofar as individual salvation is concerned... It is not in the domain of an Arahatta to know all, an honour reserved only for the Buddhas due to their immense aeonic travail.

As for ceto-vimutti (the involuted method of release) it is given as in the text. There is no other method. We feel called upon to belabour this subject, because it is essential to realize that the seat of consciousness, the life-continuum, the heart-base (as distinct from the peripheral mind with its centre in the brain) has its function in the centre of the diaphragm. If the peripheral faculties are not *consciously* sunk to this life-continuum base (as they are *unconsciously* done in sleep) nothing really worth knowing about 'self' and 'not-self' will ever be revealed. And why? Because it is in the life-continuum, not in the immediate brain, that antecedent (rebirth) data are registered and stored. It should be understood that the Eightfold Path (condensed under the steps of Sila, Samadhi, and Panna) is not merely a peripheral exercise or abstraction, but is something to be cultivated (bhavana) and integrated at the life-continuum base in the centre of the diaphragm It is through the door of this centre that consciousness finally becomes integrated and intense, so as to reveal depths unplumbed before.

However, emphasis should not be directed at the nostril or the eye apertures, because if so progress will be slow. We have to bring down the peripheral centres to the seventh position, and push on from there... As for walking etc., it is good to be mindful. However, it is wearying and unrewarding to direct attention only at the bodily movements, and this should not be carried too far. What is of import is that whenever you are walking, sitting, standing, or lying down, to concentrate attention at the seventh position, in the sphere there, whether with eyes opened or closed. The sixth and seventh positions are the most vital of centres, and

46

thinking and investigation of the Dhamma should be investigated there for the most beneficial results. Facility in this keeping of the attention at the seventh position will eventually be attained with continual practice.

Regarding the position of the elements, it should be understood that as given in the diagram they are merely visual aids. As a matter of fact, the size is really nucleic, and they are inextricably mixed and do not exist in isolation at all. What is of importance to know is that the elemental nuclei are impermeated by a cognitive base, otherwise the organism would not function. In the earth element there is the water element etc., in the water element there are the other elements, and so on, the proportions differing only in degree. The elements are distributed throughout the organism and it is only a question of which element predominates at a given moment. If any one element is in excess the balance is disturbed. Thus, if the fire element is in excess the metabolism of the organism is upset, and fever is the result. Too much significance should not be placed on the elements, for as the Master has said:

"Both the personal and external elements are to be regarded as they really are, by perfect insight: this is not mine, not this am I, herein is not the self of me. So regarding them, one is repelled by them and cleanses one's heart thereof."...

Those who have never practiced deep concentration before are only too ready to pass an *opinion*. As the Master said to Vacchagotta, the dhamma is hard to see and understand, rare, excellent, subtle, to be comprehened only by the wise:

"To you it is difficult, who have other views, another persuasion, another belief, a different allegiance, a different teacher... A thicket, a wilderness, a tangle, a bondage and fetter of views, attended by ill, distress, perturbation, fever, not leading to tranquillity..."

Regarding the elements, it is to be understood that the external elements we perceive around us are different in composition from that of the organism, because inorganic existence is not impermeated by a cognitive base. The organism is impermeated by such a cognitive base because the rebirth consciousness supplied

47

the foundation by impregnating the cell in the mother's womb. From thence the cell sprouted into two, two into four, etc, until the fully developed organism was complete. If there was no cognitive base, the development process would never have started to sprout its offshoots. That is why it is said that each nucleus of the four basic elemental (organic) structure is impermeated by a cognitive base, because that is how it all began...

Some people may descend to the seventh position according to the facility whereby they are able to induce it by preliminary techniques, such as in-and-out-breathing, etc. It is of no consequence, so long as the peripheral faculties eventually arrive there. There is, of course, no sense in trying to *force* one's way down there, because it will be unrewarding. The idea is to let the faculties sink of their own accord to that point, to gradually induce them to. This is done everyday when one is about to sleep, without any amount of force but by *nature*. For one cannot force oneself to sleep, one only tries to *induce* it. It is strange that everyone does this everyday by nature, and yet is unable to do it by an act of self-volition. The only difference between sleep and the volitional way, is that the former is done unconsciously whereas the latter is something to be done by a direct technique, accompanied by full awareness. Therefore, try and observe what happens when one is about to doze off.

You are right to say that when you want to put your mind anywhere you just direct it there. The process is automatic, and that is how the mind works. Basically, what is seen is the first nucleus (Pathama Magga). To see other nuclei, which there are, the process will have to be directed to dead centre of that first nucleus. But this is most difficult to achieve, and entails an expansion of the first nucleus to spherical dimensions and a very keen penetrative insight, which is only developed with time. Of course, your efforts are not wrong or in vain, though in the beginning one may be beset by difficulties. But then all things excellent are as difficult as they are rare.

As for the sixth position, it is the most difficult of all to understand, for that is the seat of the collective subconscious life-continuum (bhavanga) and contains all the impressions (sankharas) pertaining to antecedent experience. It is to the sixth position that the peripheral faculties sink and gravitate when sleep descends

48

(without a dream) and the sensation is of sinking as into a void. When the faculties arise to the seventh position, then dreams arise. Therefore, to try and get to the sixth position in full awareness is something which only the adept is proficient at. It is more fundamental than the seventh position, because it is at this juncture that the embryo fused in the mother's womb. When the untrained faculties are sunk at the sixth position they know nothing, flowing on just like a river. To take cognizance of anything, the faculties have to edge up a step from this subconscious - continuum before anything can be cognized, and that is the significance of the seventh position...

Regarding the matter of the Mahayana and Theravada ideals. It was good to hear that you have the Bodhisatta ideal at heart, because the world would surely be a better place in which to live were all to have such an outlook. However, it is important to understand that when the rebirth - aggregates are extinguished and the Nibbanic plane attained, one ceases to be a Bodhisatta but becomes an Arahatta or a Buddha, as the case may be. Since an Arahatta or Buddha in the Nibbanic plane knows no more rebirth, he can no longer aid creatures across to the other shore, for he possesses a physical form no more, as to make himself visible. It also should be understood that each Buddha has only a limited following, and this is so because the extent of influence is fixed as such, no more. This disposes of the theory that Buddhas are capable of putting off their Nibbana for an indefinite period until all creatures have been saved. We, of course, do not say that past Buddhas and Arahattas in the Nibbanic plane are incapable of aiding creatures who supplicate for aid. But the aid transmitted is of an imperceptible nature and far too subtle for the normal person to definitely determine. The task of a living Bodhisatta, on the other hand, is to influence (although not fully enlightened himself) creatures in the immediate world by direct aid and effort, so as to accumulate gradually a band of future disciples. This is his task.

Now it should also be understood that although many may aspire to the ideal of a Bodhisatta, they cannot be recognized as

49

such until they have accumulated a vast amount of preparatory parami (as given in Appendix Five of Samma Samadhi II), after which they must be accepted and predicted as such by a Buddha of that period wherein the vow is verbally made. Only then are they classed as fully-fledged Bodhisattas whose vows possess the certainty of fulfillment. There are some who originally started to build the paramis, but later, after still having a further term to serve, renounced their vows (because of the vast amount of time and effort involved) to become ordinary Arahattas.

Thus, although in theory anyone may aspire to be an All—Enlightened Buddha, the matter is not so feasible in actual practice, because of the vast amount of resources and ability necessary to support the vow so as to fruition in actualized reality. We do not say that men should not aspire, and lack of resources does not make aspirations null and void, because even if All - Enlightened Buddhahood is a protracted affair, even an ordinary man possesses the capacity to influence his fellows, no matter in how limited a sphere. It must be understood, however, that the sphere of influence of any given personality depends upon his own spiritual *weight*, which like a stone thrown into a lake causes concentric ripples to expand under the impact, to an extent in proportion with the gravitational weightiness of the stone itself.

What is more, the paramis are never on any account rendered extinct with the attainment of the Nibbanic plane. It is the weight of the paramis which fulfill aspirations and make the attainment of release possible at all, whether for self or a multitude. We must not confuse merit (punna) with perfection (parami), because one who has attained to Arahattaship or Buddhahood has nothing further to do with punna, having passed beyond, but parami is a thing of essence and is a Buddha's and Arahatta's actual being, something without which he can neither exist or act as a Buddha or Arahatta. Any action (or non - action) of a perfect one is only an external manifestation of his internal resources called parami, and distinguishes him as such...

The whole matter of the so - called Mahayana and Theravada ideals has been greatly exaggerated and overemphasized, causing a deplorable split, an offence of the first magnitude, as Buddha's reprimand to Devadatta bears witness. There is no basic distinc-

50

tion between the two, for there is no 'higher - greater' or 'lower - lesser' path, there is only *one* path. Because whether in the attainment of that path one goes alone or takes others also, it is in Nibbana, not elsewhere, that the path ends, no more. The true Bodhisatta is one who does not exploit his aspirations as a platform, but who toils and travails in retiring humility for the sake of universal welfare. Only this is his goal, only this his reward. As Santideva consoles himself :

"Thus through all the good accumulated by me, may I become a tranquillizer of all the pains of beings."

THE GOOD SEED

(Twelve in Brief)

But others fall on good ground and grow, and make up for the lost seed, and bear ears which fill and yield thirtyfold, sixtyfold, and a hundredfold.   No mortal hand makes it, but the seed itself swells, sprouts, and puts forth leaf, stalk, and ears that fill with grain.

JOSEPH OF EGYPT
(c 1500 B. C.)

A seventeen year old shepherd boy wanders out of the vale of Hebron, in the land of Canaan, in search of his brothers. The best loved of Jacob's sons, he is envied by his brothers because of this.

Wandering among the hills and valleys the boy Joseph reaches Shechem, where his brothers are supposed to be looking after the flocks. But they are not to be found, and he wanders on in search. A stranger whom he meets says that they have gone on to Dothan. To Dothan, therefore, he wanders on.

But when his brothers beheld him coming from afar, they decided to slay him and throw him into a pit, for in their eyes he was a dreamer of dreams. They stript him of his coat and threw him into the pit. But when merchantmen on their way to Egypt passed by, the brothers changed their minds, drew him out and had him sold.

As a consequence of which, Joseph was eventually sold to Pharaoh's captain of the guard, Potiphar, and because of his character and ability came into great favour thereby. However, rejecting the seductions of his master's wife, he was falsely accused out of spite and sent to prison.

But even in prison he was preserved, and found favour with the keeper thereof.

Now at that time it came to pass that Pharaoh's butler and baker were also cast into prison, and both having dreamt dreams, Joseph interpreted them. Thus he came to be known to them as an interpreter of dreams.

When Pharaoh himself dreamt a dream, therefore, the boy Joseph was sent for to resolve it, since no one in the land could do so. And Joseph foretold that according to the dream there would be seven years of plenty, following which famine for seven years would ravage the land. Thus during the seven years of plenty corn must be stored up to tide over the seven lean years.

55

Because of the wisdom displayed, Joseph grew into great favour in the eyes of Pharaoh, so much so that he was moved to exclaim: Where can we find such a man as this? Wherewith Joseph was made chief minister in the land.

During the seven plenteous years Joseph saw to it that corn was gathered in and a fifth part thereof stored in the barns, until they were full. Then the seven years of famine struck. But in Egypt there was bread. When the people of Egypt came to Pharaoh for aid, they were told to go to Joseph. And he sold them Pharaoh's stock.

From all over the neighbouring countries they came. And out of Canaan so did the brothers of Joseph, and bowed before him, as Joseph had once dreamt they would. He recognized them all, but they knew him not. And he feigned roughness in his speech. But when he overheard them whispering among themselves of their past guilt in wanting to slay him, he turned away and wept.

Joseph eventually made himself known to his brothers, after first sending all his servants out of the room. Then he wept After which he said:

"Do not be angry and grieved at yourselves. I am he whom you sold into Egypt. It was no fault of yours, for it was not you who sent me. I was sent here by a great Providence to preserve life, and to save your lives by a great deliverance. Go back and bring my father and come here to live. For two years has famine ravaged the land, and there are still five more years to go. Haste you and return."

He sent them away with sackfuls of corn, and returned their money in the mouths of their sacks. And when they brought their father back with them, Joseph made provision for them all in the land of Goshen, for the rest of their days.

As the famine waxed sore all over the land, Joseph sold corn to all, and delivered the money to Pharaoh. When money failed, the Egyptians brought their goods and cattle in exchange for corn. Finally, when even that failed, they sold their land to Pharaoh.

And Joseph made a law, that since the land was now Pharaoh's, seed should be given the farmers with which to sow the land. Four parts of the crop would be theirs (one part for seed,

56

one for food, one for the household, and one for the little ones), and the fifth part would be Pharaoh's. And the people were content with this as a just law, in gratitude saying:

"You have saved our lives! Now let us find grace in your eyes!"

And Joseph lived to be an old man, to 110 years of age, and died in Egypt.

LAO TZU
(c 600 B. C.)

"He who is ever a slave to desire can see no more than its (Truth) outer fringe... All things have a source, even as rivers from some far off fountain spring. To find this source needs concentration of mind, refreshing and unfolding in endless supply. As one concentrates, the eye divine appears, and lust and greed depart... There is one thing in the universe which the eye sees not, nor the ear hears, nor the mind grasps, yet by meditation is realized. Though we look up its brightness is not perceived, nor is it seen when we look down. There is no adequate name for it, everpresent though it be. But as the mind by concentration becomes unified, then the mind becomes as empty open space. This is what is meant by the form of the formless, the image of the imageless... As the mind becomes motionless at this extreme and abides serene, it returns to its state pristine. For who is there that can make muddy water clear? But if allowed to settle, it will clarify. Thus it is that without moving you shall know, without looking you shall see, without doing you shall achieve."

This is so because without moving out of doors the whole world may be known, without gazing out of the window the way of heaven may be seen, the further one travels the less one may know. However, the sage too moves unsettled as the sea, drifting as though he has no resting place. Nevertheless, solitary as he is and unlike the rest, he revers Tao, that path which the layman does not know.

"My words are very easy to understand, very easy to put into practice. Yet the world can neither understand nor practice them.

57

My words have a clue, my actions possess an underlying principle.
It is because men do not know the clue that they understand me
not. Thus the sage clothes himself in coarse garments but carries
in his heart a gem."

Tao remains, continues its work, inexhaustible, slowly
transmuting and perfecting all things until each is ripe. In Tao all
things are produced, its virtue nourishes them all, each formed
according to its nature, each perfected according to its strength.
The law of Tao is its own spontaneity.

Although Lao Tzu made little impression on his contempor-
aries, he nevertheless left a legacy of spirit which inspired the
centuries which ensued, and prepared the way for that typical
poetic identification with the spirit of nature which is to be found
in the records of the ancient Chinese.

In his later years the sage left his home and books for good,
and wandered out into the open country of the Chinese West. It
is conjectured that he was on his way to India, there to visit a
greater sage. But that great one (Buddha) had already passed away.

And the old one himself was heard of no more.

PLATO
(427 - 347 B . C)

After returning from travels abroad, in Sicily and Egypt,
Plato established the first Academy in Athens, where through the
medium of personal contact his following grew. However, it is in
his writings that he remains alive.

Plato's chief concern was the search for truth and the wisdom
mind. But this search is impeded by the mind itself, which is like
a charioteer with a pair of winged horses, one of which is of noble
breed and the other ignoble, and therefore the driving is necessarily
difficult and hard. Through the conflict the mind is either drawn
downwards or soars upwards. When it is nourished by beauty,
wisdom, and goodness it grows apace. But when it feeds on evil
and ugliness it wastes away and is destroyed.

"Every seeker after wisdom knows that his mind is a helpless
prisoner, chained hand and foot in the body, compelled to view

reality not directly but only through its prison bars, and wallowing in utter ignorance. And wisdom can see that the imprisonment is ingeniously affected by the prisoner's own active desire, which makes him first accessory to his own confinement. Wisdom takes over the mind in this condition and by gentle persuasion tries to set it free, pointing out that observation through the eyes and ears and all the other senses is entirely deceptive and urges the mind to refrain from using them unless it is necessary to do so, and encourages it to collect and concentrate itself by itself, trusting nothing but its own independent judgement upon objects considered in themselves, and attributing no truth to anything which it views indirectly as being subject to variation... The mind of the true philosopher feels that it must not reject this opportunity for release, and so it abstains as far as possible from pleasures and desires and griefs, for this is the worst calamity of all. Because whensoever the mind feels a keen pleasure or pain it cannot help supposing that whatever causes the most violent emotion is the plainest and truest reality, which it is not. It is through this sort of occasion that the mind passes most completely into the bondage of the body."

If true happiness is aspired to, a man must live the good life. He must live it, and not just talk about it. Because:

"The subject does not admit, as the sciences in general do, of exposition. It is only after long association in the great business itself and a shared life that a light breaks out in consciousness, kindled so to say by a leaping flame, and thereafter feeds itself."

The noblest of all studies is the study of what man is and what he should pursue. And what should he pursue?

"A man must have intelligence of Universals and be able to proceed from the many particulars of sense to one concept of reason. Of Universals there are three which are of prime import: Beauty, Truth, and the Good. When rulers have reached fifty years of age and have experience, the time has arrived for the final task: to raise their eyes to the universal light which brightens all things and behold the Absolute Good."

This is so because the Form of the Good is the most difficult of forms to perceive:

In the world of knowledge the Form of the Good is perceived last and with difficulty, but when it is perceived it must be inferred that it is the cause of all that is right and beautiful in things, producing in the visible world light and the lord of light, and being itself lord in the intelligible world and the giver of truth and reason. And the Form of the Good must be perceived by whosoever would act wisely, whether in public or in private."

To achieve his goal a man must possess self-control and courage, for the mind is too easily debased by pleasure and by pain:

"Every pleasure and pain has a sort of rivet with which it fastens consciousness to the body and pins it down and makes it corporeal, accepting as true whatever the body certifies. The result of agreeing with the body and finding pleasure in the same things is, I imagine, that it cannot help becoming like it in character and training, so that it can never get clear away to the unseen world, but is always saturated with the body when it sets out, and so soon falls back again into another body, where it takes root and grows. Consequently, it is excluded from all fellowship with the pure, and uniform, and divine."

It is of first importance, therefore, to discipline the mind.

"To withdraw from all contact with the body and concentrate itself by itself and to have its dwelling, so far as it can, both now and in the future, alone by itself, freed from the shackles of the body."

This is so because the mind which is freed of the body is like a brilliant eye:

"When resting upon that on which truth and being shine, it perceives and understands, and is radiant with intelligence. But when turned towards the twilight of becoming and perishing, then it has opinion only and goes about blinking, and is first of one opinion and then of another and seems to have no intelligence."

Plato died at the age of eighty, while attending a wedding party of one of his pupils. Amidst the din he had retired alone to another room to rest. When they found him he had already passed away.

60

MARCUS CATO
(95 - 46 B. C.)

Orphaned at an early age, the character of Cato suffered little from this loss. On the contrary, even as a boy he was known for his firmness of mind and could not be intimidated by fear. The times in Rome were so corrupt that Cato, already austere by nature, was at pains to live the life of virtue. With this end he, after becoming a priest of Apollo, studied moral and political science under Stoic philosophers. Although he studied oratory, he was reserved by temperament and was blamed for his reticence. But to this charge he replied:

"Men may blame me for silence, but I hope not my life. I will begin to speak when I have that to say which had better not be left unsaid."

Later, in his public life, he could speak on matters of import for a whole day without stop. Study and retirement, however, was his chief occupation. Physically, he inured his body to labour and went bareheaded in all seasons and often walked without tunic or shoes. When he became tribune and was given command of a legion he disciplined his men in virtue and won their admiration and love, so that when his term expired they were so sorry to see him leave that they wept and, laying their cloaks at his feet, kissed his hand as he passed, a signal honour not accorded to even commanders - in - chief.

After this, Cato travelled east to increase his knowledge before he returned to Rome. Back in Rome he plunged into politics and attained great prestige in the senate because of his moderation and justice. He was always the first to arrive and the last to leave. After this, Cato's life was occupied in struggling to prevent either Caesar or Pompey from assuming dictatorship in Rome. Until finally the struggle between these two ended in the death of the latter. Cato himself retired to Africa in dejection at the imminent crumbling of the republic, and from that day never cut his hair or shaved his beard, nor ever lay down except to sleep.

Earlier, on the pleadings of an admirer, he had given away his wife. Now on the death of this friend he received his wife back and delivered the care of his children to her, while he himself set sail for Africa. In Africa he saved the lives of the inhabitants of Utica, whom Scipio wished to put to the sword for having taken Caesar's side. But Cato protested vehemently against such a barbarous act.

Cato's humanity never showed itself better than in his last days in Africa, as he tried to save the people from Caesar's wrath. A second time he saved the lives of the Uticans, when Scipio's soldiers wished to destroy them. Says Plutarch:

"Every class of men in Utica could clearly see, with sorrow and admiration, how entirely free was everything that he was doing from any secret motives or any mixture of self-regard. He who had long before resolved on his own death was taking such extreme pains, toil, and care only for the sake of others, that when he had secured their lives, he might put an end to his own. For it was easily perceived that he had determined to die, though he did not let it appear."

Cato's last hours were memorable. At supper amongst friends that night talk fell on philosophy, namely, that the good man alone is free, and all wicked men are slaves. Cato argued his point wtih great vigour, until it became apparent to all that he intended to put an end to his life rather than fall under the tyranny of Caesar. After this, there was a great silence and dejection.

When he retired for the night, he lay down to read Plato's dialogue on immortality. Then missing his sword, he asked for it, but no one stirred. Then his son and his friends beseeched him not to take his own life, but were unable to prevail against his resolve. His sword was then given him by a boy, and testing its point he was satisfied, saying that now he was his own master. He then lay down again to read Plato, which he did twice over. After this he slept so soundly that he snored. On awaking, he inquired if all those who had escaped by sea were safe, and was told that the wind was high and the sea rough. At which he sighed in compassion for those at sea.

He then fell again into a light slumber. His servant returned to report that all was now quiet at the port. Then Cato, making as if he would sleep the rest of the night, told him to shut the door after him. As soon as he found himself alone, he stabbed himself in the breast. But his aim was faulty and he did not immediately die, but fell struggling to the floor, the noise of which brought in all the household. They stood aghast, for his bowels were out and he was yet alive, staring at them. His physician made to put in his bowels and sew it up, but Cato recovering himelf pushed him away, and plucking them out again, immediately died.

The people of Utica hailed him as their benefactor and saviour, the only free and undefeated man, and although Caesar was marching on them, attended his funeral with great pomp and buried him by the sea. Cato was forty eight years old when he died. And they built a statue to his memory by the sea.

JESUS OF NAZARETH
(4 B. C. — 29 A. D.)

The good spirit is like grain, and its essence is sown in the world even as a farmer sows grain in his field.

"He sows over the whole field regardless where it falls. And some seeds fall by the wayside, and the birds of the air come and eat it up. Other seeds fall among stony ground, and though they sprout up they wither in the blast, because there is no room for their roots. Others again fall among thorns, and as soon as they arise are choked thereby. But others fall on good ground and grow and make up for the lost seed, and bear ears which fill and yield thirtyfold, sixtyfold, a hundredfold... No mortal hand makes it, but the seed itself swells, sprouts, puts forth leaf, stalk, and ears that fill with grain. Only when it is ripe does the farmer send reapers to gather in the harvest... After the farmer has sown good seed in his field, he rests. As he is resting, the enemy comes and sows darnel in the field."

So Jesus of Nazareth in the fields of Israel. Already at twelve years he had discoursed with the elders in the temple of Jerusalem forgetful even of his parents in the greater business at hand. At thirty years, out of Galilee, by the river Jordan, and on into the desert, where after forty days and nights of fast and vigil the power of the spirit grew great in him. Then the open field.

63

But no one understood.

"Except you see signs and wonders you will not believe!"

If signs there were, the time was short, and the hour of darkness nigh wherein no man could work. So when his disciples prayed him to eat, they were told that he had meat enough. For his meat was to finish his work fast, and not for them to say that the harvest was afar off, for the fields were white already to harvest. And he who reaps receives his reward, for he gathers fruit into eternal life, that both the sower and the reaper may rejoice together.

"The harvest truly is plenteous but the labourers are few. Pray you, therefore, that the lord of the harvest send forth more labourers into the harvest... Therefore say I unto you: take no thought for your life, what you shall eat or what you shall drink, or what you shall wear. Is not the life more than the meat, and the body more than the raiment? Behold the birds of the air, they sow not, neither do they reap, nor gather into barns! Consider the lilies of the field! how they grow: they toil not, neither do they spin. And yet I say unto you that not even Solomon in all his glory was arrayed as one of these. Take, therefore, no thought for the morrow, for the morrow shall take thought for the things of itself."

In the villages and towns, Jesus of Nazareth went about, preaching to those with eyes to see and ears to hear. And he was seized by a great compassion for beings because they perished without knowing the truth, and troubled and tormented themselves without knowing why, like scattered sheep who have no shepherd.

But shepherds may be found who are ready to die for their sheep. For the good shepherd gives up his life for his sheep. And why? Because if a grain of corn fall not to the ground and die, it remains alone. But if it die, then it brings forth much fruit.

But no one understood.

"All things come to life by understanding, and without it nothing can live. Understanding gives true life and is the light of truth. And the light shineth in darkness. But the darkness comprehendeth it not."

64

MARCUS AURELIUS
(121 — 180)

In Rome, in Asia Minor, or by the Danube, the emperor - philosopher viewed the world with a mixture of melancholy resignation and calm distaste.

"Of human life the time is a point, and the substance in flux, and the perception dull, and the body subject to decay, and the mind in a whirl, and fortune hard to divine, and fame a thing devoid of judgement. And, to say all in a word, all that pertains to the body is a stream, and all that pertains to the mind a vapour and dream, and life a warfare and stranger's sojourn, and after fame oblivion. What then is that which is able to conduct a man? One thing only, Philosophy."

At the age of eleven he garbed himself in coarse garments, as Stoic philosophers garbed themselves, and practiced austerity and abstinence until it almost ruined his health. The adopted son of the emperor, no sooner did he come to the throne then his reign was beset by wars which occupied his attention off and on until his death. But a wise man does not complain.

"Time is like a river made up of the events which occur, and a violent stream. For as soon as a thing has been seen it is carried away and another comes in its place, and this will be carried away too... Unhappy am I because this has happened to me? Not so, but happy am I though this has happened to me, because I continue free from pain, neither crushed by the present nor fearing the future... One man buries another, and is himself buried in a short time. Observe how ephemeral and worthless things are, and what was yesterday a little mucus, tomorrow will be a mummy or ash."

What then to do?

"Be like the promonotory against which the waves continually break, but it stands firm and tames the fury of the waves around."

How does this apply to the mind?

"Such as our habitual thoughts, such also will be the character of your mind, for the mind is dyed by its thoughts. Things themselves do not touch the mind, nor have admission there, nor turn or move it. The mind turns and moves itself alone and whatever judgements it may think proper to make, such it makes for itself of the things which present themselves... Dye the mind, therefore, with a continuous series of thoughts such as these: that where a man can live there he can also live will. If he live in a palace then he can also live well in a palace. For whatever purpose each thing is constituted, towards that it is carried... Look within! Let neither the peculiar quality of anything nor its value escape your mind... Above, below, all around, are the movements of the elements. But the motion of virtue is in none of these. It is something more divine, and advancing by a way hardly observed, it goes happily on its road."

The wise man has no room for conceit, for all is vain.

"Some things are hurrying into existence and others are hurrying out of it. And of that which is coming into existence part is already extinguished. In this flowing stream, on which there is no abiding, what is there then on which a high price can be set? It would be just as if a man should fall in love with a sparrow which flies by, but it has already passed out of sight! Take care that you are not made into a Caesar, that you are not dyed with this dye, for such things happen. Keep yourself simple, good, pure, serious, free from affectation, a friend of justice, kind, affectionate, strenuous. Reverence the gods and help men."

And always:

"Look within. Within is the fount of good, and will even bubble up if you only dig... How then shall you possess a perpetual fountain? By forming yourself hourly to freedom, conjoined with benevolence, simplicity, and modesty... The mind free from passions is a citadel, for man has nothing more secure to which he can go for refuge... It is in your power to live free from all compulsion in the greatest tranquillity of mind. Short is the little which remains to you of life Live as on a mountain. Let men see, let them know a real man who lives according to nature. If they cannot endure him, let them kill him, for that is better than to live as men do."

Perception of elements and analysis of forms.

"Examine into the quality of form and detach it altogether from its material part and contemplate it. Then determine the time, the longest which a thing of this peculiar form is naturally made to endure... A man deposits seed in a womb and goes away, and then another cause takes it and labours on it and makes a child. Again, the child passes food down the throat, and another cause takes it and makes perception and motion and life and strength. Observe, then, the hidden things which are produced in such a hidden way, and see the power just as we see the power which carries things downwards and upwards, not with the eyes, but still no less plainly... The healthy eye ought to see all visible things and not say: I wish for green things, for this is the condition of a diseased eye. Remember that this which pulls the strings is the thing which is hidden within... In contemplating yourself never include the vessel which surrounds you and these instruments which are attached to it. There is no more use in these parts without the cause which moves and checks them."

A man lives well in that he does things for the general interest.

"Let this always be present to thy mind and never stop doing good. Guard against four aberrations and wipe them out thus: this thought is not necessary, this tends to destroy social union, that which I am going to say comes not from my real thoughts, these pleasures are gross."

And, lastly, the spirit of intelligence, which is above all.

"When you are troubled you forget how close is the kinship between a man and the whole human race, for it is a community, not of a little blood or seed, but of intelligence... The spherical form of the spirit maintains its figure, when it is neither extended towards any object, nor contracted inwards, nor dispersed, nor sinks down, but is illuminated by light, by which it sees the truth, the truth of all things, and that truth which is in itself... These are the properties of the natural spirit: it sees itself, analyzes itself, makes itself such as it chooses, enjoys the fruit it itself bears, and obtains its end wherever the limit of life may be fixed. It is sufficient in itself, for in whatever part it may be stopped it is full and complete. It traverses the whole universe and the surrounding vacuum, surveys its form, extends itself into the infinity of time, embraces and comprehends the periodical renovation of all things, and knows that those who come after will see nothing new, nor have those who were before seen anything more. A man who is forty years old, if he has any understanding at all, has seen by virtue of the uniformity that prevails, all things which have been and will be. Also the property of the natural spirit is love for its neighbour, truth, and modesty... See what things are in themselves, dividing them into matter, form, and purpose. Man is composed of body, breath, and intelligence. The first two are ours insofar as our duty is to take care of them. But the last alone is properly ours. Separate it from the impressions of sense to which it is attached, past and future, *and make itself into a sphere, all round, and in its joyous rest reposing by itself pure and free.*"

The Emperor died in 180 near Vienna, having contracted a contagious disease during the German campaign. And his ashes were returned to rest in Rome.

SANTIDEVA
(691 - 743)

Santideva, a prince of Surat in India, is said to have been persuaded in a dream to renounce the throne of which he was heir and to become a monk. He became the pupil of Jayadeva, the Abbot of Nalanda, the renowned university of the name.

During his life Santideva was concerned chiefly with one thing, the ideal of bodhisattahood, the ideal that a man must work without let for the salvation of all beings. And the first thing to that end is the development of the wisdom - mind (bodhicitta). This it is quite possible for a man to do.

"One can accomplish all aspirations having gained the life of a human being, which is hard to gain."

The wisdom - mind is like a flash of lightning in the night, encompassed by the dark of ignorance and evil. One has to exert oneself aeon after aeon and discover the gem which does not perish, and which saves all beings. The number of those who exerted themselves to save beings in the past is beyond counting. They have constantly engaged themselves in the welfare of others by day and night. However, they do not mortify the body without purpose, because a fit body can do much work for the benefit of beings. But they are ready to sacrifice even their lives and limbs as opportunity affords. This is how they go from strength to strength and how their merit accrues, the end-result of the greatest of efforts.

"Even as there is no movement when the wnid lies still, even so no merit accrues without the wind of will."

But effort alone is not enough. It must be channelled by concentration of mind. Thus it is necessary to retire into solitude to tranquillize the mind and to attain to concentrated insight (vipassana). In the caves and moonlit woods there is tranquillity.

"When shall I retire to a sequestered spot and meditate under a tree. Trees are not disdainful things, therefore shall I associate with my charming friends the trees. Delighting in the woods and regardless of life, no robber would rob me of my priceless bowl and robe."

Life is but a dream, thousands of them. The eye of truth is hard to gain, all around disbelief is to be found. To be born a human being, at a time when the Buddha word is still available for study and practice is difficult indeed. But being born well, let the earnest man put sensuality to rout and, raising himself above hardship, raise others too as well. Man goes from suffering to suffering and knows it not. But the earnest man strives to do good and tranquillize the pains of all beings.

"When to them that are burnt in the fires of pain shall I through my favours born from the rain - clouds of my merit shower peace? When shall I to them who look upon things as real the void in reverence teach? Thus through all the good accumulated by me may I become a tranquillizer of the pains of all beings."

KUKAI (KOBO DAISHI)
(774 — 825)

On top a mountain the greatest Japanese saint Kukai, after having gone to China in 804 returned to establish in 816 his monastery of Koyasan, where he painted symbols, wrote, and taught.

69

Kukai's task was to search in all the doctrines prevalent for the truth and to see in what quantity and quality it existed in each, and thereby to bring them all into a synthesis of unity. Already in his youth he had studied Lao-Tzu and Confucius. Then in 793 he became a monk. Taking his refuge in nature, he retreated to the mountains and facing the great Pacific meditated in the face of great temptations. When he was 24 years of age he attained to a degree of insight. Then in China he absorbed the wisdom of the great sage Keika, who on his death-bed told him to return to Japan and spread true Buddhism there From China, Kukai brought back hundreds of volumes into which he delved.

"Numberless are scrolls of learning. In some are the surface teaching, in others the deep. The beginner does not know where to begin. What is to be gained by reading them all? Not to be plumbed by reading is the true life. Darkness enshrouds the seeker after truth on all sides. Blindly all creatures flounder on from life to life through the three realms of existence, born over and over again, but gathering no gain. The light remains unseen. Who shall lift the veil of darkness and death in which all drown?"

Only a Buddha is able to do so. And the Buddha is the Dhammakaya, which has form and speech. Unlike all other sects of Buddhism, which consider the Dhammakaya as formless and silent, the Shingon sect which Kukai founded recognized that the Dhammakaya is with form and speaks.

The result of all his vast research and experience was to resolve all doctrines and minds in ten grades, each having its part to play in ascending scale in the evolution of man:

(1) animal man and his appetites
(2) the morality of a Confucius
(3) the mentality of a Lao-Tzu
(4) the mind aware of its own amorphous plurality
(5) the passionless mind
(6) the mind filled with the thought of liberating others from pain
(7) the mind purged of illusion reaches the middle path between two extremes
(8) the mind in search of true identity
(9) the liberated mind
(10) the mind with perfect knowledge of all things

Kukai distinguished universal life as Ideal and as temporal. The Ideal world is termed vajira-dhatu (diamond element) in that it is indestructible. The Buddhas belong to this category. From this Ideal proceeds the wisdom which saves the world, and it has five attributes:

(1) the knowledge of the evolution of beings
(2) the knowledge of all elements
(3) the knowledge of non-differentiation
(4) the knowledge of law, of good and evil
(5) the knowledge of duty, which leads to the salvation of all

The temporal world, termed gabbha-dhatu (primordial element) is the universe of earth, water, fire, air, and space. But although for matters of analysis universal life may be divided thus into two, it really interacts as one, differing only as to modes of static and dynamic, the esoteric and the exoteric.

Not only did Kukai during his lifetime paint, write, and teach, as well as have temples built, but he also built schools for the poor, invented a Japanese alphabet, and even built a reservoir in which waters could be stored to supply farmers in times of drought.

Kukai, having completed what he set out to do, it is said that he gave orders for them to bury him (after he had gone into meditation) alive. This was in 825. Thus concluded he his earthly sojourn.

FRANCIS OF ASSISI
(1181 - 1226)

Francis Bernadone, born among the hills of Assisi in Italy in 1181, after having attained manhood, left the world and practicing abstinence and poverty attracted twelve chief disciples, one of which eventually hanged himself.

Alone on an uninhabited island in Lake Trasimeno in Perugia, he (Francis) sought shelter in a dense thicket and began to pray and meditate for forty days and nights, consuming only half a loaf of bread during all that time.

Fortitude was a virtue which occupied a prominent place in the eyes of Francis Bernadone. Once as he was walking along the Perugian road with his disciple Leo in front, it being winter and very cold, he began to discourse on all the virtues, concluding however that all of them no matter how good they were, still were not the source of perfect joy. For almost two miles he kept on in this negative chant, until the exasperated disciple would know indeed what was the source of perfect joy.

"The source of perfect joy is this. When we arrive at our destination soaked with rain, stiff with cold, covered with mud, exhausted with hunger, and when we knock at the friary door and the porter beats and kicks us out into the rain and snow, hungry and frozen, and if we bear it all with patience and calm, without complaint, that is the source of perfect joy. Above all graces and gifts, that of the grace of fortitude and conquest of self stands out. And why? Because these gifts belong to no one but are our own. All else we possess is given us, but this cross of suffering and affliction we may glory in because it is all our own."

Even in his lifetime Francis of Assisi acquired a great following. So much so that his disciple Masseo tried to test his humility in this respect, saying "Why after you, why after you?" When Francis inquired in perplexity what he was trying to say, he made his meaning clear.

"I mean, why is it that the whole world is following you, and why does everybody want to see you, hear you, and obey you? You are not handsome, you are not very learned, and you are not of noble birth. Why, then, does the whole world want to follow you?"

On hearing this, Francis was uplifted with a strange joy and went into a trance. When he returned to himself he knelt down and gave praise.

"You want to know 'why after me'? You want to know why the whole world is following me? It is because of the marvellous work that can be accomplished by a poor sinner like me. For a poor sinner can in this way he lives confound the nobility, greatness, power, beauty, and wisdom of the world. Showing that virtue does not proceed from any man but proceeds from above, for that is its source."

72

Francis sent out his disciples to preach by pairs. One day as he himself was walking with Masseo they came to a crossroad. Masseo inquired which way they were to take. Francis told him to spin himself round and round and not to stop until he was told to do so. Masseo spun round so long that he began to grow giddy and fell. But he got up and spun himself again, because he was not ordered to stop. Only when he was spinning around fast was he ordered to stop.

"In what direction are you facing?" inquired Francis.

"Towards Siena."

"Then that is the road we are to take."

As they reached Siena, they were met by the populace with great display of affection and carried on their backs, so that they set no foot on the ground. At that moment they met certain men fighting, two of whom were already killed. Francis spoke to them and healed the discord, reconciling the combatants. The Bishop of Siena entertained him, but Francis and his disciple rose early next morning and left without the Bishop's knowledge, desiring to escape all honour. Masseo was puzzled in his heart why he had been told to spin around at the crossroads and why they were now leaving in haste But he was made to realize later that a great deed had been done, for by coming to Siena many lives had been saved.

Francis himself was dubious as to his mission, whether he was to spend the rest of his days in solitude and prayer or to go out and preach. Having gained a large following he asked his disciples for advice in the matter. After much deliberation and prayer they came to the conclusion that he had been sent into the world not for his own salvation but that many through his example might be saved. Hearing this, Francis set out and preached. He preached with such favour that those who heard him wished to leave their homes and follow him. Which he forbade them to do, making them lay disciples instead. He became so fervent that when he saw flocks of birds in the trees, he was struck with wonder at their beauty and began to preach to them on the virtue of gratitude. It is said that the birds flew down and listened in silence with open beaks, with stretched out necks bent low, displaying their delight, until he having finished they soared up in song into the sky.

Once together with Masseo, Francis arrived in a town. Famished they went separately to beg in the streets as was the rule. As Francis was poor looking and short he received only a few morsels and crusts of dry bread. Masseo, however, due to his good looks and height received whole loaves of bread. They met again outside town to eat beside a beautiful spring. On a fine broad rock they laid out their meal. Francis was overjoyed to see that Masseo's collection was better than his, exclaiming aloud over and over again:

"O brother Masseo, we are not worthy of so great a treasure!"

But Masseo was not impressed, for he saw no treasure, not even a knife or dish, or table or house, or anyone to wait on them. But Francis consoled him.

"That is what I call a great treasure, where nothing has been provided by human labour, but everything has been given by divine providence. Let us love this treasure of holy poverty which is so noble."

Having been donated a hill in Tuscany by one Orlando, a lay disciple, Francis taking with him three disciples, Masseo, Angelo, and Leo, went up this lonely and wild Mount La Verna for their retreat to practice great austerities. Finding even deeper solitude, Francis left his disciples behind with orders not to follow him, and retreated to pray in the moonlit woods. It was then that he received in his hands and feet and breast the stigmata, the five wounds of Jesus of Nazareth.

A few days before his death, as he lay sick in Assisi, Francis often sang. This scandalized his disciples, afraid lest the layfolk on hearing him might think him mad. So Francis was carried away from Assisi. On the way he told them to lay him down on the ground and face the city. He blessed the city, saying that through it many would be saved.

He died in 1226, on Saturday the 3rd of October. After which the movement he had established took the world by storm.

WILLIAM SHAKESPEARE
(1564 — 1616)

"What is a man if his chief good and market of his time be but to sleep and feed? A beast, no more. Surely he that made us with such large discourse, looking before and after, gave us not that god - like reason to fust in us unused."

The Elizabethan age was as frivolous as any age. Given such an environment it is difficult for any serious minded man to make himself heard. Profoundest convictions have to be veiled in the guise of entertainment so as not to displease. Even as the age of Plato so the age of the Stratford sage. The only respite from frivolity is in the forest.

"Hath not old custom made this life more sweet than that of painted pomp? Are not these woods more free from peril than the envious court? This life exempt from public haunt finds tongues in trees, books in the running brooks, sermons in stones, and good in everything."

Would it not be better, then, under the shade of melancholy boughs, to lose and neglect the creeping hours of time? For all the world is a stage, and life a shadow play, where the actors soon melt into air, into thin air.

"And like the baseless fabric of this vision, the cloud-capped towers, the gorgeous palaces, the solemn temples, the great globe itself. Yea, all which it inherit, shall dissolve, and like this insubstantial pageant faded leave not a rack behind. We are such stuff as dreams are made on, and our little life is rounded with a sleep."

But men will continue to be lured by a fantasy and trick of fame and go to their graves like beds, fighting for a plot whereon the numbers cannot try the cause, which is not continent enough to hide the slain. Let a beast be lord of beasts, and landed man spacious in the possession of dirt. As for passion, when the blood burns how prodigal the soul lends the tongue vows, giving more light than heat. The sage lifts up his eyes into the night sky, for while this muddy vesture of decay doth grossly close man in he cannot see or hear celestial things.

As for the life to come, whether this is the be-all and end-all here, nothing is known. But one thing is certain, even right here and now upon this bank and shoal of time. That is: we still have judgement here, that we but teach bloody instructions which being taught return to plague the inventor. This even-handed justice commends the ingredients of our poisoned chalice to our own lips. Since this is so, only one thing remains, mercy.

"'The quality of mercy is not strained, it droppeth as the gentle rain from heaven upon the place beneath. It is twice blest, it blesses him that gives and him that takes."

Goodness indeed is rare, but when it does appear is light whereby one may see afar. Finally, a man considers that everything that grows holds in perfection but a moment, and this huge stage presents nought but shows. And since there is nothing left to do, thus bids adieu. And all the rest is silence.

BARUCH SPINOZA
(1632 - 1677)

" After experience had taught me that all the usual surroundings of social life are vain and futile... I finally resolved to inquire whether there might be some real good... I perceived that I was in a state of great peril and I compelled myself to seek with all my strength for a remedy, however uncertain it may be, as a sick man struggling with a deadly disease.. All the objects pursued by the multitude, not only being no remedy that tends to preserve our being, but even act as hindrances. "

Against the flat green landscape and bright sky of the Dutch countryside Spinoza reflected, a solitary figure and dark. His peril was not merely physical, although one dark night he was almost stabbed by a religious fanatic, but chiefly the state of a man with no sure refuge. What, then, the remedy, the real good?

" The chief good is that he should arrive, together with other individuals if possible, at the possession of a character which is

76

stable, which has the knowledge of the union existing between the mind and the whole of nature."

First, however, it is necessary to understand that man is not as free as he thinks he is, and can do whatsoever he likes.

"In the mind there is no absolute or free will, but the mind is determined to will this or that by a cause, which has also been determined by another cause, and this last by another cause, and so on to infinity. Men are mistaken in thinking themselves free, their opinion is made up of consciousness of their own actions, and ignorance of the causes by which they are conditioned. Their idea of freedom, therefore, is simply their ignorance of any cause for their actions."

What then must a man do?

"It is before all things useful to perfect the understanding, or reason, so far as we can, and in this alone man's highest happiness or blessedness consists. Indeed, blessedness is nothing else but the contentment of spirit which arises from the intuitive knowledge of nature. The more the mind knows the better it understands its forces and the order of nature, and the more it understands the order of nature the more easily it will be liberated from useless things. This is the whole method."

The power of the mind when trained is supreme and controls all emotions. It is therefore the aim to attain to such a mind.

"Whence it appears how potent is the wise man and how much he surpasses the ignorant man, who is driven only by his lusts. For the ignorant man is not only distracted in various ways by external causes without ever attaining to true acquiescence of spirit, but lives as it were without knowledge of himself and nature and of things, and as soon as he ceases to suffer, ceases also to be. Whereas the wise man in so far as he is regarded as such, is scarcely at all disturbed in spirit, but being conscious of himself and nature and of things, by a certain eternal necessity, never ceases to be, but always possesses true acquiescence of spirit."

Of all things, understanding of the nature of things sets the mind free from fear.

"A free man thinks of death least of all, and his wisdom is a meditation not of death but of life... These and similar observations, which we have made on man's true freedom, may be referred to strength, to courage and nobility of character... These propositions all relate to the true way of life and religion: that is, hatred should be overcome with love, and that every man should desire for others the good which he himself seeks. Wherefore he strives before all things to conceive things as they really are, and to remove the hindrances to true knowledge such as hatred, anger, envy, derision, pride, and similar emotions. This he endeavours as far as in him lies, to do good, and to go on his way rejoicing."

And in conclusion:

"If the path I have shown to lead to this is very difficult, it can yet be discovered. And clearly it must be very hard when it is so seldom found. For how could it be that it is neglected by all if salvation were close at hand and could be found without difficulty? But all things excellent are as difficult as they are rare."

Spinoza died on Sunday the 21st of February 1677 at the age of forty four.

LEO TOLSTOI
(1828 — 1910)

Already when he was twenty - seven years of age Tolstoi, a soldier in the midst of the Crimean War, was seized by a stupendous idea 'to the realization of which I feel capable of devoting my life'. This was nothing other than to 'deliberately promote the union of mankind by religion'.

Already in childhood, a boy of five, he believed in the existence of a little green stick, supposed to be buried at the edge of a certain ravine, a stick whereon was said to be written the secret message whereby all evil in men could be destroyed and give them universal welfare. In his childhood, too, he had already come across pilgrims of faith, and their image remained fixed in his memory.

"Much water has flowed since then, many memories of the past have lost their meaning for me and become dim recollections, but the impression these pilgrims made on me and the feeling evoked will never die in my memory."

78

Then the death of his brother Nicholas (who told him the tale of the little green stick) made a deep impression on his mind.

"It is nearly a month since Nicholas died.   That event has torn me terribly from life.   Again the question: Why?   Already the departure draws near.   Whither? Nowhere!.. He died literally in my arms. Nothing in my life has so impressed me. Wise, good, serious, he fell ill while still a young man, suffered for more than a year, and died painfully, not understanding why he had lived and still why he had to die...   Be useful, be beneficient, be happy while life lasts, say people to one another.   But you, happiness and virtue, and utility, consist of truth.   And the truth I have learned in thirty two years is that the position in which we are placed is terrible.   As soon as a man reaches the highest degree of development, he sees clearly that it is all nonsense and deception."

But recourse to Nature strengthens faith in life

"On my way back in the evening twilight I rode through Turgenev's wood, Spasskoe.   Fresh grass underfoot, stars in the sky, the scent of blossoming willows and dead birch leaves, the nightingale's notes, the sounds of cockchafers and cuckoos—cuckoos and solitude—and the brisk pleasant movement of the horse under me, and physical and spiritual health.   And I thought, as I constantly do, about death.   And it was so clear to me that on the other side of death it will be as good, though in a different way, and I understood why the Jews represented Paradise as a garden. The enjoyment of nature is the purest form of enjoyment.   It was clear to me that there it will be just as good, and better."

Tolstoi tried and tested himself in many ways, to see how much he could stand.   A close observer at that period notes:

"He was never saner than at this period.   He was testing internally and externally just how much he could endure and how hard it is to do without this or that thing.   Of course, only those nearest to him could know this...   He took up these manias only in the spirit of penitence, to subdue the flesh and elevate and enlighten his spirit.   There was even a time when he really seemed to wither up and become thin.   Any one who noticed how his narrow belt was continually being tightened a hole or two could easily have convinced himself that this too was one of the paths to salvation.   Yet at the same time he was good - natured and often merry... It happened at times that he threw off from himself Leo Tolstoi the writer, the Count, the shoemaker, the aristocrat, the father of a family, and became simply himself, for he possessed the capacity of throwing off one skin after another, like an onion."

He abandoned flesh meat, alcohol, and even tobacco. But terrible was the fight:

"He suffered unendurable torment, positively not knowing what to do with himself. He would pick up a cigarette - end here and there like a schoolboy, to have but a single whiff, or dilating his nostrils he would eagerly inhale the smoke when others smoked in his presence."

He and his daughters with some young folk worked in the fields, harvesting in the hay, working till sunset, hasting to finish the job. And as they rested, Tolstoi would tell them tales of good and evil. In answer to the question whether there could be life without evil, he said:

"Man comes of good, not of evil. Here is a legend. The lord thought of a creature to create: But the angel of truth said: create him not, he will defile your temple. The angel of justice also said: he will be cruel and love only himself. The angel of peace said: he will steep the earth in blood. The lord's face became overcast with doubt. But the angel of mercy, his youngest and best loved child, came forth, saying: create him! when all your servants leave him, I will find him, help him, and change his shortcomings to good. I will guard him that he stray not from truth, I will draw his heart to sympathy and will teach him to show mercy to the weak. And the face of the lord grew bright: Live! breathed he, and know that thou art the child of mercy. That is how mercy was created, and yet you say man is the outcome of evil!"

And he smiled. The afterglow of sunset was fading. And he delivered a last legend to suit the mood:

"A king's daughter is betrothed to a man who gives her everything. But she remains unmoved. And why? Because she is a king's daughter, and has always had everything. So it is with the spirit. Earth spreads all her treasures before it and strews its path with carnal pleasure. But it remains cold and unmoved. And why? Because it is of heaven."

80

They parted in deep thought. The meaning of the legends, the tone in which they were told, and the whole atmosphere of labour and faith imprinted indelibly on the mind as something unusually joyful and elevating.

When Tolstoi was 63, famine threatened the Russian countryside. Said he: "Have you heard? It has already begun. They have nothing left to eat and are already sitting idle in their homes. It is the first groan of an approaching calamity. I feel it, and ache inwardly, as a rheumatic body aches before rainy weather."

For two years Tolstoi engaged in famine - relief work, establishing and supervising the running of 246 eating - houses in which ten to thirteen thousand people were fed, also another 124 kitchens for children where two to three thousand fed.

"It is excellent food!" said the peasants. "God bless the good Count and all his friends for giving us such good meals. What would we have done without him? We never want better food than this!"

But after two years of relief work Tolstoi was a weary man, weary of the endlessness of human misery. They came on and on to his door, saying:

"We have not eaten for two days. We have sold our last sheep. What are we to do? Must we die?"

To them their sufferings were new, but to him they were as ancient history.

"Yes, it has wearied us. But they still want to eat, still desire to live, and still long for happiness and love."

In Tsarist Russia peasants were regarded as little better than animals. Tolstoi not only championed the poor, but spoke out fearlessly against the corruption of the times. One observer declares:

"In these dark days, days of ominous social silence, when it seemed as though all that was alive and could protest had been crushed, the solitary but powerful voice of Leo Tolstoi rang out like a bell. In artistic as well as in publicist writings he ardently protested against the oppression and exploitation of the labouring

81

masses by the strong, the ruling, and the rich, and against violence of all kinds. executions, taxes, prisons, and war."

Tolstoi's definition of religion:

"True religion is a relation accordant with reason and knowledge, which man establishes with the infinite life surrounding him, and is such as binds his life to that infinity and guides his conduct... I do not believe my faith to be the one indubitable truth for all time, but I see no other that is plainer, clearer, or answers better to all the demands of my reason and my heart. Should I find such a one, I shall at once accept it."

Tolstoi died at the age of eighty-two, on the 20th November 1910, a few minutes after six at dawn. The funeral procession was a mile long, but there were no speeches or ceremonies, only sobs as the crowd knelt down when he was put into the earth.

He was buried in the spot surrounded by nine oaks, where the little green stick was supposed to lie. The little green stick on which was supposed to be written the secret message whereby all evil in men could be destroyed and give them universal welfare.

Lightning Source UK Ltd.
Milton Keynes UK
UKHW021228170522
403091UK00003B/372